Turn Your Idea Into a Hit Reality-TV Show!

Barb Doyon

INTRODUCTION

This book is written to help anyone who's ever had an idea for a reality-TV show turn that idea into a sellable show to present to Hollywood. It's written in laymen terms so anyone can take learn to create a professional presentation, for little or no costs, that will attract the attention of producers.

The book's author, Barb Doyon, is the owner/founder of Extreme Screenwriting, a Los Angeles based coverage service for feature screenplays and TV pilots. She is a produced screenwriter, TV writer, producer, director, author and ghostwriter. She has ghostwritten for dozens of reality-TV shows and has assisted hundreds of clients with preparing reality-TV show presentations for game shows, documentary series, monster series, investigative series, paranormal series and more.

This book can teach anyone how to get an idea, package the idea, and market the idea to Hollywood. Think big because your idea could become the next hit reality-TV show!

Barb Doyon is also the author/filmmaker of the following:
Extreme Screenwriting: Screenplay Writing Simplified (Vol. 1)
Extreme Screenwriting: TV Writing Simplified (Vol. 2)
Dead Border (Feature)
Eternal Hologram (Documentary)
Zook's World (Children's Edition Book)

Available on Amazon.com
extremescreenwriting@mail.com
www.extremescreenwriting.com

TABLE OF CONTENTS

CHAPTER ONE

GET STARTED

✤ IT BEGINS WITH AN IDEA

Do you have an idea for a reality-TV show? Or would you like to learn how to come up with ideas for a reality-TV show? If you answered YES to either of these questions, then this book is for you.

Unlike feature films and TV's episodic dramas that require screenplays and TV scripts written by professional writers in the entertainment business, reality-TV can be written, presented and sold by ANYONE and this book will show you how to get the idea, craft the idea into a simple presentation and even how to market the reality-TV show concept to Hollywood.

It doesn't matter if you're a hairdresser from Cleveland or a boxer from New York. It doesn't matter if you live in a small town in Missouri or in a big city like Los Angeles.

It doesn't matter if you have no money to get started or have money to invest in a presentation package. This book will show you how to prepare the idea for a reality-TV show to market to Hollywood using little or no money and with no prior entertainment industry experience.

✤ WHAT DO YOU NEED TO GET STARTED?

It all starts with the idea or what is referred to as the <u>concept</u> in Hollywood. In other words, what's the show about?

○ Ideas are all around us

Ideas for reality-TV can come from restaurants, cafés, bus depots, stores, eccentric people, unique places, mysteries, monsters, the paranormal, food, clothing, vehicles, competitions, travel, recreation, animals, unique employment, exotic hobbies, little-known occupations, dangerous jobs, dirty jobs, global adventures, local intrigue, etc. The list of possibilities is endless, but it all starts with an idea.

    o Passion to Stick With It

If you think Hollywood's your ticket to a million dollar payday, then I'd suggest you play the lotto because the odds of landing a million bucks is more in your favor at the lottery booth. Having a reality-TV show certainly has the potential to be financially lucrative, but if you're just in it to get rich then get in the lotto line.

However, if you're tired of your 9-5 job and would love to tell the boss to take a hike, then let that be the passion that drives you because having a reality-TV show could possibly get you out of your day job! It won't be easy and will require hard work.

You may already have an idea that's churning in your mind and you can't wait to learn how to mold it into a viable presentation to sell to Hollywood. That's fantastic! Make sure it's something you can live with day after day because these shows are a full-time commitment. If you're just starting to come up with ideas for a reality-TV show, listen to your instincts. Is there a concept that jumps out at you and keeps you up late at night because you're so excited about its possibilities? That's the idea you should go with. Passion is key to staying grounded to the concept for the long haul.

    o Willingness to Devote the Time

Putting a reality-TV package together can take time. How long depends on you, but it won't be done overnight. And if you're already working a full-time job and have family obligations, I'd recommend committing a few hours during the week and on the weekends to working on the package until it's completed. Putting together a reality-TV package is like anything else in life; you get out of it what you put in to it.

Set a deadline. This will help you focus on putting the package together in a timely fashion, while learning how to meet deadlines, which will be required for the show once it sells.

○ A Computer to Put the Presentation Together

Hollywood has HD cameras, sound booms, film crews, etc., but none of those are required to put together a presentation package. All that's needed is a computer or a way to type up a presentation package so it looks professional when pitching it to the entertainment industry.

PITCHING is nothing more than telling a
producer what your reality-TV show is about.

While the presentation package is all that's necessary to adequately pitch a project to Hollywood, you might also want to consider putting together a visual presentation piece (trailer) to accompany the written pitch package. For that, all you'll need is a cell phone camera (preferably HD) and a computer. We'll talk more about putting together trailers, sizzle reels, etc., to use as a visual tool alongside the presentation package and how to do it at a very low cost, but remember the visual tools aren't mandatory for making a sale. They're optional tools to help get an idea across to a producer.

The only item that's mandatory is the Reality-TV Presentation Package.

❖ DO YOU NEED A REALITY-TV SHOW PRESENTATION?

Yes! First, what is a reality-TV package presentation? It's simply a presentation that shows a Hollywood producer, often referred to as a show runner, what the show's about, who will be on the show, what type of show it is, format (1-hour or 30-minutes) and anything that might determine if it has an audience for the producer to give the show a slot on a primetime network or cable TV.

Some presentations are only one-page long, but others can expand up to 15-20 pages and include photographs and pertinent show information. It's basically a written presentation of the show and this book will help you determine how long the final presentation will be.

The presentation package is important for two reasons:

1. It makes you think through the concept to make sure it's strong enough to sell as a reality-TV show.
2. It confirms to the producer that the show has legs and can attract an audience.

Can You Verbally Pitch a Reality-TV Show Idea?

Yes, but only if you have a presentation package to accompany the verbal pitch. A straightforward verbal pitch isn't accepted in Hollywood unless you're an established and working writer in the industry. You'll need the presentation package to get your foot in the door. It's your calling card that says you know how to be a player in this industry.

The Presentation Package is
A Calling Card to the Industry

Many of you might think this is a waste of time. Why can't you just tell a producer what the show is about and have the producer give the idea a green light or pass? Because a verbal pitch doesn't show the producer what it's about and anyone can make anything sound good, but will the concept actually work once it's fleshed out on paper? That's the real question they want answered and it's your job to put together an effective presentation that helps them see the show in their minds as a viable, commercial option they can bring to a targeted audience. This book will teach you how to put the presentation package together in a way that will help attract producers to the project.

And I'd highly suggest having more than a verbal pitch for the following, important reasons:

1. You can't copyright an idea, so just verbally pitching an idea to anyone who will listen, including producers, is the same as giving it away.

2. A written pitch can be registered with the Writer's Guild of America (WGA) and it can be copyrighted, which protects your show's concept from sticky fingers.

3. I've found that producers will often pass (turn down) a reality-TV show pitch because the show's Creator (that's you!) doesn't really know how to present the material verbally, but the Creator left the presentation package with the producer for future consideration. I've seen more than one show sell this way! Don't be embarrassed, it's tough to get up there and pitch a concept in front of producers. Don't worry if you're the shy type because I'm going to teach you how to pitch and sell a show via the Internet, YouTube, and other sources. Or how to use parts of your presentation package, like the trailer, sizzle reel, etc., to sell the show for you!

4. Having a written reality-TV presentation package puts you in the game and allows you to pitch the concept anywhere, anytime to anyone and market it worldwide 24/7. Imagine selling a reality-TV concept while you sleep! This book will show you how!

Have Fun With the Presentation!

Don't let the fact that you'll need a presentation package intimidate you! This book is going to show you how to put it together from the ground up and how to simplify it so anyone can do it! Think of it as a new adventure in life that's has the potential to take you where you want to go by living life on your terms, working on what you love and possibly never having to undertake a day job again.

You can keep the presentation to one page or expand it out into trailers, sizzle reels, photographs, scripts, a multi-page presentation, etc. Deciding what is the best way to present your package is up to you, but this book allows you the option to go simple or elaborate. Whether you decide to go with a one-sheet presentation or the full package, I'd recommend you read the entire book to familiarize yourself with how a complete presentation package is put together. After your first sale, you'll have funds and be able to put together other packages for presentations and have multiple shows on the air. I've seen it happen!

Don't be fooled into thinking the bigger your presentation package is the better your chances at selling a concept to Hollywood. That isn't necessarily true. While I believe the trailer and sizzle reel are certainly powerful because they provide a visual representation of the show, I've seen a written presentation package sell just as fast because the concept was entertaining and presented in a way that helped it draw the attention of show runners.

Finances aren't a consideration since I'm going to show you how to put together a presentation package for $0. I'm betting most of you think putting together a trailer or sizzle reel is out of your league because you're familiar with the movie trailers we've all seen and know cost tens of thousands or even millions of dollars to make, but the reality of a reality-TV show is that a simple 30 second to 1 minute trailer can be put together for as low as $300 to $1K. I know many Creators of shows who've put together trailers and sizzle reels on a shoestring budget. And this book will show you how to do it too. If that's still too much, it's okay. I'm going to make this presentation become a reality for you even if you don't have a dime to spare.

❖ HOW ANYONE CAN SELL A REALITY-TV CONCEPT

We've all had ideas for a reality-TV show, whether the idea came from our aunt's donut and hamburger café or from the eccentric neighbor down the street who put together a street gang to develop alternative energy sources. Or maybe there's an unsolved mystery in your town. Because ideas are all around us, it doesn't matter if you live in rural America or New York City. You can sell a reality-TV show to Hollywood!

Most of you have good ideas, but don't know how to put the ideas together in a way to present to the entertainment industry. This book will show you how to build the hype required to go viral with the concept and Hollywood will be hot on your tail to purchase the show and put it on the air!

It doesn't matter if you already have a full-time job; part-time job or you're unemployed. This book shows the average person how to put together a presentation with no money; a low- budget or the sky's the limit. Any one of the presentations could appeal to the entertainment industry. Yes, it will take some leg work and you'll have to devote the time and effort into putting a reality-TV package together, but for little or no cost, and maybe a few weekends of work, you could potentially sell a show to Hollywood, even if you've never worked in the industry and even if you don't know anyone in the industry. The old adage that it's who you know in the entertainment industry doesn't hold true for reality-TV. You can be virtually unknown and sell a reality-TV concept. In fact, Hollywood will probably find it even more exciting that you came out of nowhere!

Use This Book Like a Manual

First, I'd recommend you have a reality-TV show in mind. Decide what kind of reality-TV market best fits your series. Would it make a great game show, a documentary-series, or a half-hour show? If you don't have a concept in mind, but would like to come up with something in the future, read through the chapters and see if anything from real-life can fit into the markets and presentation packages outlined in this book.

When producers first started hearing pitches for reality-TV, they purchased ideas and developed them into shows. That's no longer the case. A pitch has to come in a packaged form, ready to be filmed (or already filmed) and ready to go to TV. Even if you're just pitching from a presentation, the concept has to be planned and ready to go!

Next, pick the budget that best suits your needs and bookmark that chapter. Read through the chapter for an overview of what you'll need to do to present the concept to the entertainment industry. Later, I recommend you read through the other chapters to get ideas for putting together future presentation packages when you have more funds available.

Third step is to create a game plan that involves a schedule and deadline for putting the package together. Be realistic and stick to the deadline. This will help prepare you to meet specific deadlines should the show sell, assuming you're interested in staying on with the show rather than just doing an outright sale and walking away. It's a far more lucrative prospect to stay aboard for the show's duration as its creator collecting residuals (more on this later).

The Person who comes up with the Original
Story Concept is called the show's Creator! That's you!

Follow the book's instructions for the budget and complete the presentation package. Now you're ready to hit the market. Continue the instructions and see who bites in Hollywood. Reality-TV shows are red hot! There's a good chance producers will contact you even before you've contacted them and that's a rarity in Hollywood, just ask any aspiring screenwriter or TV writer. While they've waited months or even years to get a response from Hollywood, you could have producers contacting you on a daily basis! Or you can market to them directly, unlike screenplays and TV pilots that are often turned away with a note reading 'no unsolicited material': producers welcome reality-TV, but you need have a presentation package to solicit producers directly.

Insider's POV

Creating a presentation package is the easy part, but you'll need insider information on how things operate in the world of reality-TV. Don't assume you know because you're a reality-TV buff who watches every new show. How these shows are put together might surprise you. For example, did you know some are scripted and some even use ghostwriters! Others might be staged while some are shot off-the-cuff. We'll discuss all of the different ways shows are put together in this book.

It's important to know the ins-and-outs of this unique form of entertainment. Being informed from the get-go will help you put together the best presentation, assure you get a fair market price, will help you understand your rights and responsibilities as the show's Creator and help you decide if you want to do an outright sale where you walk away and let someone else run things or if you want to be a more hands-on Creator who stays for the duration of the show and reaps all the rewards it has to offer.

This book can also help you steer clear of pitfalls from the presentation through the end of a series. The first thing to understand is what's real and not real about reality-TV.

❖ IS REALITY-TV REAL?

One of the shocking aspects of reality-TV is that some of it isn't as real as it appears to be. SPOILER ALERT! This section gives away insider information regarding specific shows. While this information has been printed in other public formats – so it's not really a secret – most reality-TV fans are unaware of the reality of their favorite shows.

For example, when the show *House Hunters* hit the market, it was an instant hit, but the producers ran into a problem when the show's participants ended up not qualifying for the house they'd selected, so the producers, rather than cancel the show, reinvented their approach to the show by pre-qualifying the participants. This means the participants already know which house they qualified for and the other two houses are just props for the viewing audience's amusement. Some aren't even for sale, but are the houses of locals used in the show. Want to know which one the participant will pick? The one that's empty! The other two are literally not for sale! Sorry to burst your *House Hunters'* bubble, but those are the facts. The show's now taken to 'staging' houses to look lived in so it's harder for the audience to tell which one the participants will select. AND, the show's producers run the participants through what's said...that's right, they rehearse! Ever notice how everyone wants stainless steel appliances and granite countertops? Odd because anyone with kids will tell you what a fingerprint mess it is to have stainless steel appliances that constantly need wiping down! I've never checked, but I'm guessing the show's advertisers or sponsors consist of companies specializing in stainless steel appliances and granite countertops. So much for reality-TV, it's as staged as any show on the air!

The show's not as real as it appears, but hey, the audience gets to see real houses in a specific market/location, so the show remains a hit. I'm personally shocked at how tiny the places are in Europe. It makes me glad to be a homeowner in the USA! It's a cool show, but it's close to 100% staged! Don't take this wrong. Those are real people seeking a real house and the show helps them find it and helps with their expenses, but the future occupants are pre-qualified and the rest is staged.

There are shows that claim to never 'fake' anything, like *Duck Dynasty*, but I've personally heard they reshoot the interview portions on a regular basis when they don't go quite right. Many shows script, rehearse, shoot and reshoot the interview portions. That's the part where one of the show's cast speaks in a sidebar fashion to the audience for informative purposes, gossip purposes or just to tell us how he/she is feeling about something that's happened in the show; these sidebars are often written by ghostwriters.

Documentary-series, like *Ancient Aliens*, while subjective, have the strongest base in reality because they're put together with factual and/or opinion information that's presented in an entertaining format, usually in a one-hour show. All the interviews are scripted and portions of the show might be reshot to get the right tone, mood and atmosphere for the series. The exception might be shows that spontaneously collect information as they go along, like

Ghost Hunters and *Finding Bigfoot*. While these show's Creators have maintained a level of integrity by refusing to put misleading information into their shows, similar shows on the market, while based in collected factual information, often present it in a suggestive way that could mislead an audience to one conclusion or another.

Then there's the character shows like *Little Women of L.A.*, *Housewives of Beverly Hills* (or wherever), while they'll debate how 'real' they are, take a look at the credits for yourself. You'll clearly see part is scripted, probably the interviews. In fact, if you're wondering about your favorite reality-TV shows, check the credits. Is there a credit for script editor, story consultant or anything along those lines then it's a fully or partially scripted show. The exception is Script Supervisor, which is a continuity person. This person makes sure everything is the same in a feature film or TV show during various takes of the same shot within a scene, like the actor's tie was crooked in one scene, so the continuity person (Script Supervisor) makes sure it's crooked in all the takes. Of course, if you see this credit on a reality-TV show, then that means scenes are shot over and over again . . . so much for reality.

As I mentioned above, even if a show's shot for REAL, once it gets into post production and it's edited, it can be spliced to slant a story in many different ways. Again, this brings the 'real' part into question.

Regardless, reality-TV is the hottest trending market. People love to watch ordinary people's lives unfold on TV. They get caught up in it and an audience will stick with it even if it's obvious it's faked. I think reality-TV will be around for a long time. I believe there are currently more reality-TV shows on, per network, than other type of show.

Beyond understanding how reality-TV shows work, the Creator will need to select the best choice for packaging and selling a reality-TV idea.

❖ APPROACHES TO PACKAGING & SELLING REALITY-TV

This book is laid out in a way to allow the Creator to select the best approach to packaging and selling a reality-TV show, primarily based on the type of packaging the Creator can put together; a zero budget package, a low-budget package or even a high budget package.

Before deciding on one, the Creator should read through all three-budget options for packaging. The Creator might decide to switch from a zero budget to low budget or even high budget package and put the financial costs on a credit card or cash in some stocks. It's up to the Creator to decide what financial risks to take.

The packages have similarities and the more you put into it, the larger the presentation and the more expensive the costs involved. In terms of selling, the more money you put into the presentation, the more likely you'll be to gain attention for the show. This isn't because you've spent more. Rather it's what you spent the money on; a trailer and a sizzle reel. By providing a visual of the show, a producer can see what it might look like and this can be extremely appealing. However, nothing beats a great concept and that can be exploited with a written presentation that blows a trailer or sizzle reel out of the water. I've seen this happen. The Creator puts together a decent sizzle reel, but a competitor, who has no reel or trailer, puts together a red-hot concept and ends up with the sale.

During the course of the book, we're going to talk more about deciding what goes into the presentation package(s) and making it happen, but I'd like to provide a word of advice before getting started. ALWAYS listen to your gut instinct. It'll never let you down.

After Creators learn how the reality-TV business works, they start to wonder if an audience will accept their concept. After all, the idea comes from a large city where ideas are a dime-a-dozen or maybe the idea comes from a small town no one's heard of. Can these types of ideas find a mainstream audience?

Hometown Reality Versus Small Town Reality

Anyone can sell a reality-TV concept from anywhere, but are ideas that come from a big city better than an idea from a small town or vice versa? After all, in the big city ideas are a dime-a-dozen, while the small town idea may be too small to appeal to a wide audience. The reality of reality-TV is that is doesn't matter. Shows from the big cities, like *Cops* have become hit series, while a show like *Duck Dynasty* also became a hit out of the backwoods of the USA.

Big City Dime-A-Dozen Concepts

Let's say you live in Los Angeles, which is a trendy city piled high with competition in the entertainment industry from acting to writing. One day you're driving along the freeway and see a chain gang working in their orange jumpsuits and think that would make a good reality-TV concept. After all, there are already several shows on reality-TV about prisons and prisoners, this just expands upon that base and takes the concept outside. It might even be more exciting to watch! So, the Creator packages the concept and does an ultra-low budget trailer. Then shops it only to find 200+ other Creators in the industry are already shopping the exact same concept! Remember that day you saw the chain gang on the freeway? Well, so did 200 other competitors! That can be a downfall when it comes to living in a city like Los Angeles or New York City because everyone's looking for the next hit show. Of course, it could be a plus if the Creator happens to run across a concept that's timely, but not likely to be mainstream. Maybe your cousin works in the Los Angeles Harbor and does security or something more localized that only you have access to. This is your best bet when coming up with a concept with a large-city slant to it.

Hometown Reality Hits a Home Run

Hometown reality has some big advantages over the big city reality because it's unlikely there are 200 others in a small town who are going to compete with your concept. However, the small town may not have much to offer in the way of reality-TV concepts compared to the big city. But take a really close look around, especially if you've lived there a long time. You might be used to Joe Smith's Catfish and Naked Dancers Club and may not realize the weird variation could make a hit reality-TV show. Drive outside your town, stop for a meal, and then drive back in with a fresh perspective, like you've never been there before. Even if you don't think there's anything worthy of a concept, try to come up with at least one thing. Is there something you can combine? Can you get Mable's Bed & Breakfast to cater to UFO hunters from a neighboring state that passes through her place once a year?

Maybe you could make it a weekly visit. The wilder and crazier the better!

Is there someone highly specialized in town, whether it is a person or a group? There's a show on the air about ironsmiths and another about people who build and prepare doomsday bunkers, food and other items for a post-apocalyptic event. Maybe your town has the only earthworm farm in the country or the growers of the last crop of golden apples. If you aren't sure, check with a local historian or your town's City Hall. Finally take that local wine tasting tour or ghost hunt. Find out information you might not have known about your town or had forgotten because you've lived there so long it simply slipped your mind.

Whether you live in a big city or a small town, this book will help the Creator determine if a concept(s) is worth spending the time to develop into a presentation package. Once a Creator comes up with an idea it's important to evaluate the idea's prime ingredient.

❖ THE KEY TO REALITY-TV

Screenwriters and TV writers will tell you it's the concept that sells the story. Is the idea interesting enough to attract an audience? Well, this isn't always the case with reality-TV. After all, what's exciting about a duck-hunting whistle? If I came to you 10 years ago and said I have a show about a family that sells duck-hunting whistles, you'd probably laugh at me and rightfully so.

Let's face it *Duck Dynasty* isn't a hit reality TV show because of the whistles. It's the **CHARACTERS**.

Characters = Key Ingredient
To Selling a Reality-TV Show

Regardless of the concept, it's really the characters that sell reality-TV. I can already hear the arguments from would-be Creators that shows like; *Ancient Aliens, Dead Files, The Story of God, I Killed my B.F.F.,* etc., are concept driven. Are they? I've actually seen similar shows shopped around Hollywood with boring scientist-types trying to sell the concept of ancient aliens, long before the famous writer of "Chariots of the Gods", Erich Von Daniken, or the hip, modern-day Indian Jones globetrotter, Giorgio Tsoukalos, stepped up to the plate and stole the show. *The Dead Files* gives a new twist to ghost hunting, but it's the chemistry of the retired homicide detective and the psychic medium that makes the show. And I doubt *The Story of God* or *The Story of Us* would have such a large audience if it weren't for its narrator, Morgan Freeman. Interesting characters sell every time regardless of the concept.

So stop looking solely for interesting ideas and start thinking in terms of memorable characters. Those duck-hunting whistle guys sell a boring product, but their wild man looks and old school ways capture and hold an audience's attention forming a committed fan base. A producer recognized this and the rest is history.

Put the concepts aside for a moment (we'll work on those later) and go back and look around your big city landscape or your small town and start picking out the eccentric, savvy, memorable or for some reason interesting characters and take note. They could be your ticket to the entertainment industry and don't worry about whether or not they'd want to do a show. We all know that everyone wants to be a star!

Throughout the chapters in this book we'll take a more in-depth look at recognizing, finding, soliciting and contracting with characters (real-life people who will star in your reality-TV show) and how to get them aboard for the production, even if at first they're a bit camera shy.

Don't worry if you only have an idea right now. For now let's stay focused on the key selling point and take a look at how interesting characters are used to sell shows. Memorable characters can be good guys, villain types, eccentric-types, loners, naggers, gossipers or even virginal types, etc. It all depends on the show. Game shows are a case in point.

Characters & Game Shows

If the Creator's concept involves a competition show, maybe it's a bass hunting competition show for the Animal Channel; it's still the characters that will eventually be the main selling point.

Think about the phenomenal success of shows like *Survivor*. How many times can we watch people getting kicking off the island and one man or woman winning a million bucks? You'd think we'd be tired of it by now. Such a concept should have faded long ago. Maybe it did, but we keep coming back because we get hooked into the characters, their stories and each season we pick our favorites and watch to see how they'll place in the game. It's also a show that brings out the best and worst in people: the villains and the good guys. And guess what, we love it because the CHARACTERS lock us in and sell the concept.

Shows that have ignored the personal side of the equation have either never made it on the air or have had a very short shelf life and rightfully so because it's characters that sell a reality-TV show.

If the Creator has a concept, but hasn't really recognized the importance of the character angle, don't worry. We're going to combine these two during the course of the book and teach you how to package the two into a viable reality-TV show.

For some shows, a celebrity host might do the trick and this book will teach the Creator how to attract talent to a project and get them signed and on board.

The Celebrity Touch

Regardless of what type of show you're selling, a celebrity touch never hurts. Don't worry, this isn't mandatory, but if you discover that Sam Elliott grew up in your small town or the character actor Michael Madsen went to elementary school there or Julia Robert's sister, a hairdresser, lives and works there, why not solicit the celebrity with your concept to see if her or she might be interested in being a regular on the show, hosting the show, narrating the show or maybe just doing a quick walk-on to bring publicity to the show? You don't have to be a big Hollywood producer to solicit them because you're appealing to something personal that they may connect with on a visceral level and want to be a part of. If not, then thank them for their time and package the concept without them. Don't be surprised when the show takes off and they contact you and have changed their mind about making an appearance.

By the way, having a celebrity in the package doesn't guarantee a sale. This might sound gross, but you're more likely to sell a concept about an earthworm farmer that actually eats live worms and runs a yearly contest to determine who can eat the most worms before you'd sell a show about Michael Madsen going to school in the earthworm's farm town. Got it? It's all about characters that hold certain uniqueness in one form or another! The celebrity may or may not add a magic touch to the show. If they do, then pitch the show to them. If not, pass them by and go for the worm eater. He's your golden ticket. Of course, if the celebrity will eat the worms, then the Creator has a winning ticket, but don't count on it.

In fact, a show completely reliant on the celebrity to sell it could be detrimental to the Creator. Why? If that celebrity decides to leave the show for any reason, it's cancelled and the Creator's show is off the air! If one of the *Duck Dynasty* guys quits that show can still go on; although I understand it's wrapping with a final season. Even if you're a fan, be happy because this means there's plenty of room for another show with memorable characters.

Memorable versus Controversial

We're going to talk in more depth about characters later, but since we just spent so much time discussing how the key to reality-TV are memorable characters, I thought it imperative to mention at this point that memorable characters doesn't mean controversial characters.

By some accounts, the *Duck Dynasty* guys might be considered red necks, but that doesn't mean your red neck show will sell if the characters have a rugged, mountainous appearance, go hunting, wear camouflage like it's Armani and shoot domestic cats and dogs to keep the local stray population down. WAIT! WHAT? They shoot domestic animals? Everything was sounding good until the concept and characters took on a controversial edge that won't sell anywhere. Cruelty to animals is extremely taboo on TV (and in film). Be sure your memorable characters aren't outrageously controversial. Unless the show is about prisoners, a show with characters who have rap sheets as long as your arm isn't going anywhere. What about the long-running *COPS* show? That show was about the *COPS*, not the suspects with wrap sheets.

My advice is to steer away from controversy and if you're not sure about your character(s) then do a criminal background check. This can be done on-line at a minimal cost. Cover your behind because the studio will check and you don't want to spend months of time putting together a package only to find out the studio and/or producer considers the character(s) too controversial to put on the air. I know there have been exceptions like *Pit Bulls & Parolees*, but it rare to get this type of show on the air unless the Creator already has multiple hit shows, then a more controversial concept can be pitched, but it's still a long shot to get it on the air.

Final Word

Use this book in whatever capacity needed to enhance, expand or even learn how to create a reality-TV show presentation package. Every aspect of this book probably won't apply to your individual concept and/or characters. Take from it what does and toss the rest. Or wait! Keep the rest for when you package a second and third reality-TV show. It's not a bad idea to have a few concepts packaged and ready to present. If a producer doesn't like the first package, he'll usually ask, 'What else do you have?' Many Creators have made a sale with their second and third concepts when they originally went into pitch a producer with the first one.

Having multiple packages available can also lead to a multiple, reality-TV deal with several shows in the works. Wouldn't that be great?

CHAPTER TWO

DETERMINE THE SHOW'S SERIES-TYPE

The first chapter provided an overview of getting started with a reality-TV idea and understanding the importance of characters. The next step is to determine the show's series type. There are different types of shows, also referred to as a 'series', and each has its own criteria. First, let's familiarize the Creator with the different types of series.

Start by browsing through the IMDB (Internet Movie Database) at www.IMDB.com under the section marked 'Most Popular Reality-TV – TV Series'. It includes every show that's ever been on the air since the inception of reality-TV, including currently running shows and cancelled shows. There are currently 12,545 titles in the database.

Don't discard the cancelled shows. Knowing what a cancelled show was about, how long it ran and when it was cancelled can give a Creator great insight into a series that might have similarities to the Creator's show, and can help the Creator avoid the pitfalls that got the original series cancelled.

Use this chapter to determine what category your show falls under, then look up and study similar shows in the Reality-TV database. We'll talk more about what to look for and how to most effectively use this information later in this chapter.

For now, the easiest way to determine the type of shows that are like yours is to find a similar show on primetime TV (big networks like CBS, CW, ABC, FOX, etc.) or cable (USA Network, SyFy, Bravo, Lifetime for Women, Hallmark, HBO, Travel Channel, Discovery, etc.). Watch the show(s) carefully and determine from the list and definitions provided below which type of show it is, keeping in mind that a show can crossover into different categories:

❖ THE COMPETITION SHOW SERIES

The Competition Show Series can run one hour or a half-hour and deal with individuals or parties competing for a prize or a reward.

They include shows like *Wheel of Fortune, Jeopardy, Hellavator, The Amazing Race, Hells Kitchen, Top Chef, Cupcake Wars, Americas Got Talent, Bachelor in Paradise, Cash Cab, etc.*

Many shows in this category will overlap with other categories. This includes shows like *The Biggest Loser* that is a competition show, but could also be considered a character-driven show. However, its primary function is a competition show, so that's its primary category.

❖ THE DOCUMENTARY SERIES

These show are usually one hour long and deal with a specific topic that are treated like a documentary with weekly episodes that deal with a sub-topic related to the main topic. For example, *Ancient Aliens* deals with the theory that ancient astronauts once visited earth. Each week the show explores places, events, facts and findings to support the theory. These types of reality-TV shows look, feel and act like a documentary with sidebar interviews from qualified authors, field specialists, experts, and include a narrator who fills in the missing pieces and moves the episode forward in an entertaining way by raising questions that the show will answer or speculate upon. This category also includes shows like, *Through the Wormhole & The Curse of Oak Island.*

❖ THE INVESTIGATIVE SERIES

Investigative shows can cover a variety of areas such as crimes (*True Crime, Fatal Vows*), paranormal investigations (*The Dead Files, Ghost Adventures*), detective-style investigations (*Catfish*), and unsolved mysteries (*The Lowe Files*).

Notice that this category often overlaps with other categories such as The Paranormal Series, The Monster Series, etc.

❖ THE PARANORMAL SERIES

The Paranormal Series often overlaps with the Investigative Series because most shows dealing with the paranormal involve an investigation to collect evidence supporting the existing of apparitions, shadow people, demons, etc. They include shows like *Ghost Hunters, Ghost Adventures & The Dead Files.*

❖ THE MONSTER SERIES

The aspiring reality-TV Creator won't find the term The Monster Series in the IMDB catalog of the Most Popular Reality-TV series, but it encompasses shows that hunt for an elusive monster. They include shows like *Finding Bigfoot, Search for the Loch Ness Monster, Killing Bigfoot, Alien Hunters, Sasquatch Mountain,* etc. Most could be sub-categorized with The Investigative Series since they involve investigations that seek out evidence of the creature(s).

❖ THE INFORMATION SERIES

These are fun shows that take us behind the scenes to places and events we might not get to see otherwise. They include shows like *House Hunters, Diners, Drive-Ins & Dives, American Pickers, Ink Masters, Pawn Stars & Undercover Boss.*

Like other reality-TV shows, they tend to overlap categories with shows like *Ice Road Truckers* that takes on a weekly adventure into the wilds of Alaska where we watch truckers literally drive over a frozen body of water to deliver vital cargo, risking life and limb. The show shifts drivers per episode and per season, but the show could still be categorized as an Information Series and a Character-Driven Series.

❖ CHARACTER DRIVEN SERIES

The Character Driven Series centers on a specific character or a group of characters and follows their stories. This type of show doesn't have a competition factor and while it may or may not have interviews, it doesn't look or feel like a documentary. This includes shows like *Little Women L.A., Housewives of Atlanta, Naked and Afraid, Keeping Up With the Kardashians*, and *Marriage Boot Camp*.

❖ CONCEPT DRIVEN SERIES

Yes, I've been harping on the key to reality-TV shows being the characters, but sometimes the concept can be the final selling point. What do I mean? Let's take a look at two paranormal shows. In *Ghost Adventures*, the three-man team of ghost hunters uses lockdown tactics to take on ghosts and gather evidence of apparitions and demonic forces. While the *Dead Files* combines the skills of a retired homicide detective with a psychic medium to weed out paranormal culprits in American households and come up with viable solutions for their removal or, if necessary, advises the homeowner to get out!

Both have very memorable characters hosting the shows and that's a definite a selling point. The three-man team of Zak Bagans and his two buddies on *Ghost Adventures* are anything but boring and a movie could be made about Amy Allen and Steve DiSchiavi's interactions on *The Dead Files*.

However, in a field that's overrun with paranormal shows, both shows broke the mold with their unique way of handling the paranormal that stood out and landed them the sale. The ability to stay on the air for so long can be attributed directly to the show's characters.

The stronger the market competition for a show, the more unique the concept will have to be to sell it. This doesn't mean an entirely new concept, but putting a spin on the old – more on this later.

Concepts Tend to Overlap

By now, I'm sure you've noticed that character driven shows often overlap with concept driven shows where having both factors in one show is a selling point. This isn't always the case for reality—TV shows, where even a duck-hunting whistle show can be a hit with the proper characters, but the whistles alone couldn't sell at a local swap meet (this reference is to the whistles as a show selling point not the product itself, which is a worldwide bestseller).

There's no real advantage or disadvantage to having one or both. Go with what works best for the show, but I am an avid believer that most successful reality-TV shows hinge upon characters the audience can identity with, care about and return to weekly to be a part of their lives.

Pick the Correct Type

Pick the correct type of show that fits your reality-TV concept, then continue reading below to discover the details you'll need to collect, research and/or bring together to package the show based on the chosen format.

Dealing with Similar Shows

TV & Film Writers knows that originality sells, but this isn't usually the case with reality-TV. In fact, there are many similar shows on the air. I've lost count of how many paranormal shows are on the air and just when I think they couldn't possibly add another Bigfoot show, guess what? They add another Bigfoot show. I've lost count how many Bigfoot shows are on the air now, 10, 15?

The trick is to give your show's premise a twist. That's why I emphasized studying the IMDB Pro database of reality-TV shows. Become familiar with shows that are similar to yours and make sure yours has an original spin.

Be careful because novice Creators can mistake original spin to mean something different when this isn't always the case. For enough to sell it. The spin isn't 'catchy' enough to draw the attention of producers. Unless of course, the location is the Mars Colony, but since we don't have a Mars Colony yet, go back to the drawing board.

The spin MUST relate to the ENTIRE concept, not just a location. The paranormal shows *Ghost Hunters* and *Ghost Adventures* do the exact same thing; they hunt ghosts. But each show has its own unique spin on how they handle the premise. In *Ghost Hunters*, the team uses practical, down-to-earth techniques and technology to confirm a paranormal presence, while *Ghost Adventures* takes it a step further by challenging the ghosts or paranormal forces and taking them head-on during a lockdown where they're literally locked in a location overnight.

Shows in this category might cast-out the paranormal, confirm the presence of paranormal activity or turn the entire show into a ghost tour. Every show has its own spin. Some have been successful while others have flopped.

First, make sure your show has its own unique spin. Next, look at who will be in front of the camera. Are the lead host and/or cast of characters interesting enough to sustain a weekly audience? I had a friend who put together an interesting spin on the ghost hunting premise, but the team he put together, while experts in paranormal technology, activity, etc., were incredibly boring. It might even be fair to say lackluster and over half the team hated being in front of the camera and it showed! I politely suggested he put the team behind the scenes as the show's consultants and bring in a more colorful cast, but he wouldn't take my advice. To this day he's never sold the show.

A colorful cast doesn't mean everyone has to look or sound like movie stars. Some might say that Si Robertson of *Duck Dynasty* isn't exactly a pretty face, but he sure is a colorful character. We all know these people in our lives from the wild and whacky hairdresser we see once a month to the mechanic who has tall family tales to tell every time we drop off and pick up our vehicles.

Or maybe it's a family member with a unique point-of-view or an oddball job.

If the show's Creator can come up with a unique spin to a type of show and mix it with colorful, camera-ready characters, then the Creator won't have to worry about how many similar shows are on the air, in development or being marketed.

CHAPTER THREE

CRAFT THE REALITY-TV SHOW

Last chapter helped identify the type of show the Creator's most interested in pursuing and determine if there's a unique enough spin and interesting characters to present the concept to Hollywood.

The next step is to start putting the show together in terms of concept, characters, locations, logistics, rules/regulations (if applicable), time frames (how long each episode will run), etc. This chapter will explore each category and what the Creator will need for that category to assure the show has the best chance at attracting Hollywood's attention.

❖ CREATE THE GAME SHOW SERIES

We all have our favorite game show and lately they seem to keep popping up with new game shows every season. Many are trivia type game shows, like *Idiot Test* or *Family Feud.* While others combine the character elements discussed in the previous chapter with a competition factor and include shows like; *Top Chef, Cake Boss, The Amazing Race, Fear Factor*, etc. What's really interesting about watching people cook? Nothing. It's the personalities behind the competition that drives the show and engages an audience. We quickly pick our favorite characters and hope they win. It becomes a built-in suspense factor that keeps the audience watching week after week. Even if a favorite contestant is eliminated, the audience quickly picks another favorite contestant and sticks with him or her until the season ends.

What's the Competition?

The Creator needs to layout the show's competition format in detail for the presentation package. How does the game work? What are the rules? Prizes? Penalties? How many participants? Is there a deadline or a ticking time clock? Is it something the audience can play along with, like a trivia show or root for a favorite character to win, like they do in shows like *The Amazing Race* or *Dancing with the Stars*?

Simplicity is Key

I've helped many clients put together reality-TV packages over the years and one of the mistakes I consistently see when it comes to game shows is the tendency to over complicate the concept, rules/regulations or to have too much going on at once. Think in simple terms or narrow the concept down to the basics. The average audience viewer is said to have a 9th grade comprehension level, which is certainly a scathing indictment of the U.S. educational system, but it rings true and keeping the show simple will assure a wider audience base. That doesn't mean making the show dumb, just easy to follow and play along. *Jeopardy* doesn't have to have its contestants travel the world to provide the question and score the points. It's done via a live studio audience with a question board, a host, three contestants and the highest score wins.

Don't Exceed the Network Limitations

If all the other TV trivia shows have a maximum prize ranging between $20k (*Family Feud*) and $1 million (*Deal or No Deal*), don't think you're clever by coming up with a $5 or $10million dollar show. These types of prizes would break the bank of any competition show with only a few payouts. Stick with the 'norm' by watching similar shows and keep prizes within those limits.

Keep prizes simple like a trip for two or a cash prize. Only have a few prizes or limit to one grand prize, if possible. This builds suspense, as opposed to having multiple prizes that different opponents win. Why? Because the audience wants to root for and cheer for a grand prizewinner!

Who Are the Contestants?

Are the contestants kids, families, a man seeking a bride, a couple vying for a prize, a group trying to win an award? Who are the contestants? Are they athletic types, soccer moms, singles, genius kids, scholars or ordinary blue-collar workers seeking a cash prize?

Don't worry if you don't have actual contestants at this point. That will come later. For now, just know what kind of contestants will be in the show.

Determine the Run Time

The easiest way to do this is to ask what game show it compares to that's currently on the air and how long does that TV show run for? Does it run for half-an-hour or for a one-hour format? Most likely yours will run the same time length.

There are several commercial breaks for each game show (for all TV shows with a few cable exceptions). It's far too complicated to try to have you understand why a commercial break takes place because it's determined by lots of things in reality-TV, such as cliffhanger moments and suspenseful moments (right after the host asks a question for final jeopardy) or it's even determined by advertisers.

There's no way for the Creator to know when or why this will happen, but it's imperative to understanding reality-TV structure. So, let's keep it simple. Watch the show that's similar in concept, style and/ or format to your show and pay careful attention to when it breaks for a commercial. What happened right before the commercial? Make sure this is a new show because reruns often have commercial breaks at a different time than the new show. You're only interested in the new show and when it breaks for commercials.

For example, in *Jeopardy*, the show breaks right after a major question for the final jeopardy portion or right after a contestant is presented with the next category. This keeps the audience watching by creating suspense. Watch and note ALL the breaks in the show and at what intervals, every ten minutes, fifteen minutes? After watching a few episodes, the Creator will notice a consistent pattern in the show breaks. FOLLOW THIS PATTERN for your show noting the competition will break right before a contestant's elimination or a prize announcement.

Beta Test the Competition Factor

I'd highly advise the Creator to get a few friends, colleagues or family members together, tell them the rules of the game and have them play, assuming it's a game they can easily play in a single setting without risking life and limb. Play the game and get feedback. DO NOT tell them it's a reality-TV concept you came up with. You want their honest feedback and they might refrain from telling you what they really think in order to spare your feelings and that doesn't do you any good. You need raw and honest feedback. Use paid strangers if you have to. Offer $10 bucks an hour for 2 hours, plus lunch and get feedback, but get it if you can. This will expose holes in the show's competition that you might not be seeing, like confusing game rules, unrealistic timelines for task completions, and even boring parts of the competition that you'll need to beef up to keep an audience entertained.

Beyond the competition, ask if they'd find this show interesting enough to watch nightly or weekly? If so, why? If not, why? What would change their minds about liking or disliking the show? Would the competition be enough to attract them or would they need a contestant to cheer for before they'd be aboard for an entire season?

Note: The participants SHOULD NOT be actual cast members at this point or contestants who might be on an actual episode. The Creator is still early in the creation phase and doesn't need to worry about casting or finding contestants at this point. For now, the Creator is just gathering information to determine if the show's a viable product that he/she should spend the time on to package and present to Hollywood.

Keep the Results

For each section noted above KEEP THE INFORMATION and/ or RESULTS. We'll be revisiting these in a later section and using all or part of the information to prepare a Concept Package Presentation!

Quick Overview

The Creator will need the following for a competition game show Concept Package Presentation:

- Write out the game's rules and regulations.
- Pick a reasonable grand prize.
- Determine the type of contestant.
- Determine the run time.
- Beta test the show.
- Keep all the results.

Keep this simple and don't feel overwhelmed. Do one section at a time and collect all the information. Don't worry if it's right, wrong, works or doesn't work. Just focus on information gathering for now. We'll check the concepts, characters and determine if the show's worthy of packaging in a later chapter.

* * * * *

✤ CREATE THE DOCUMENTARY SERIES

Documentary series are informative and usually cater to a more intellectual, knowledge seeking audience. Most viewers will never get a degree in physics, visit a super collider or travel in outer space, take a world-wide adventure to find ruins or dig for forgotten treasure, but the documentary series allows the viewer the opportunity, usually in a one-hour/weekly format to become part of this specialized world, learn from it and go on an adventure, even if the adventure is just from the armchair of a recliner.

Is the Concept Interesting & Sustainable?

Space aliens may never return to earth and the Oak Island brothers may never find treasure in the money pit. But, we all have to admit that *Ancient Aliens* and *The Curse of Oak Island* are captivating shows. Coming up with a show that can run weekly and hold an audience's attention week after week in the documentary series category can be a challenge.

There are a few things the Creator can do to assure the documentary series is interesting enough to hold a weekly audience. First, does the concept keep the audience in suspense somehow? In *The Curse of Oak Island* when the search teams see something 'shiny' at the bottom of the watery money pit: we're glued to our seats until we discover what it is. In *Meteorite Men*, the team tracks the trajectory of incoming meteorites from present day and even ancient times, but can they find the exact location? And will the landowner allow them access? The unknown keeps us guessing.

In terms of sustainability, the Creator has to be sure there's enough material to continue the series for many seasons to come. There are enough meteorites littering the earth to keep the *Meteorite Men* busy for a lifetime. *Ancient Aliens* has endless hypothesis surrounding speculation that ancient astronauts visited and influenced earthlings, to keep the show going for many seasons.

Put the concept to the test. Write out the premise and future episodes for Season One. Do you have 30, 50, or preferably up to 100 episode ideas? If not, the show may lack sustainability. Consider all the ways the show can be expanded, but remember it must stay on message even when being expanded.

Find a Budget Balance

A drawback to the documentary series can be the budget because the show's landscape often moves from state to state or even worldwide. *The Curse of Oak Island* takes place on one island, but the history of the treasure expands the globe.

Reality-TV, like all TV shows, has a limited budget. In fact, many reality-TV shows are investor funded or funded by parties outside the entertainment industry. Not all, but it's a trend in this type of broadcasting. Whether your show eventually is funded privately or via Hollywood, it will need to stick to a limited budget to make it a strong contender for a run that will last season after season.

There are ways to keep a show's budget under control. Layer the show with interviews from authors, specialists and the show's characters. Use a narrator (professional actor) to fill in vital information instead of trying to film it. Select stock footage the show can license at a minimal cost. Shows like *Ancient Aliens* takes full advantage of stock footage libraries. Watch the credits for stock footage sites listed like Getty Images, Shutter Stock, Pond 5 and others.

Extra Tidbit
Stock footage is a great way to create low budget
sizzle reels and trailers for the show.

If a Creator does these things during the creation phase, it'll show Hollywood the Creator understands how things work.

Landing Interviews

As part of the sustainability issue, the Creator will need to demonstrate he can bring in enough experts to keep the series going long term. The trick here is to build a database of experts to use over and over again on a weekly basis. *Ancient Aliens* often uses the same scientists and authors weekly to provide side commentaries on the show's topic of the week. Take the concept and start contacting experts in the field to see who might be interested in appearing on camera for an interview.

Be careful here. Everyone will say YES up front, then back down when the time comes to actually film the show. The way to weed out the ones who will leave the Creator hanging is simple. Tape an initial interview with the expert and ask questions about what they think of the show's subject matter. If the interviewee is hesitant, uncomfortable or refuses, then he/she is not a candidate for the show's 'expert' line-up. Later Chapters will cover getting release forms and contracts with the experts.

The One-Hour Format

99% of all documentary series run in a one-hour, weekly format, which is roughly 50 solid minutes of airtime after commercials. Keep your focus on creating a show of this length. In later Chapters, we'll discuss the time frame and what to do if the show is too long or too short.

Use a Test Audience

Once the Creator has a few expert interviews on videotape and stock footage selected, put it all together into a simple monologue style trailer and show it to anyone who will watch it. See their reaction firsthand. DO NOT tell them anything about the show. Just reveal the trailer or sizzle reel and learn from the feedback what works and doesn't work. If two or more of the test audience found something wrong with the concept, then listen to them! Go back and revamp those areas of the show and find a fresh group and run the test audience again.

Do not use family or friends. Use as many outside parties as possible. Maybe co-workers, a church group, card playing club, or a senior group. If you can find a group related to the show's concept, try to get their opinion up front. Be wary of the age of the group. If the reality-TV show's concept were about teen skateboarders, it wouldn't be wise to test audience the concept with seniors.

✤ CREATE THE INVESTIGATIVE SERIES

The investigative series takes a cold, hard look at the facts. The facts might stem from a crime spree; an unsolved crime, unsolved mystery, a solved crime or it can overlap with other series concepts like a paranormal investigation or a monster investigation.

Creating Suspense is Key

Suspense is a key component to the investigative series. Does the series make the audience wonder how the victim ended up dead? Or how the perpetrator escaped or how he was captured? Does the audience wonder if there really is a monster in the lake? Does the audience wonder if the missing woman will ever be found?

Raising a question creates suspense and holds the audience spellbound. They wouldn't dare turn off the show for fear they wouldn't find out what happens, especially since it's real life.

Take time to answer the questions the show raises. If the show's episode has a conclusion, like a thief going to jail in the end, then withhold this information until the very end of the episode. If the show has an open-ended conclusion, like a woman's body was never found, then make the audience wait until the end to discover that the murder has yet to be solved. Unless, of course, the show is titled *Unsolved Mysteries,* then the audience will know the mysteries remain unsolved from the start.

Inconclusive Endings & Suspense

Even if the investigative series episode is inconclusive, the Creator will need to hold the audience in suspense. Shows used to just provide the information and then end the show, but today's audience will become bored with the predictable outcome and the show won't be around for long.

Show's today have gone as far as to insinuate there might be another perpetrator out there and investigate various angles to the unsolved mystery. Perhaps one witness believes the victim must know the perpetrator, while law enforcement believes the perpetrator was a stranger.

Exploring an unsolved mystery or crime from different angles creates a natural sense of suspense because it raises questions from various viewpoints.

Investigating the Elusive Subject Matter

If the investigative series involves an elusive subject matter, like Big Foot or a Lake Monster, things can get tricky. The audience anticipates that the show isn't going to produce an actual monster. So, how does the show's Creator keep the audience in suspense and keep them coming back week after week?

Curiosity is the key. Human beings have a built-in curiosity that makes them wonder and want to explore. If the show goes beyond mere facts and presents new, never-before-seen footage, new evidence, new eyewitnesses, unexplored areas, untapped theories, etc., the Creator can lock in the audience week after week.

How is this done? One way is to tag the end of the show with a mini-trailer of next week's episode. In *Finding Bigfoot*, they show the team running across something new, exploring locations no one has gone to in years or ever, using new technologies to hunt the elusive ape; all of which creates suspense whether they find Bigfoot or not.

Is the Concept Interesting & Sustainable?

This applies to many different series, but should be looked at long-term for the investigative series. The Creator may have 1-3 ideas for the show from local crimes, but then what? Since these shows usually revolve around one investigative concept, like murder or a monster, the Creator will have to make sure there's enough material to sustain a series long-term, for many seasons.

Let's say the Creator wants to explore murders that involve a love triangle and calls the series LOVE TO DIE. Each week the Creator wants to investigate what lead up to the love triangle turning into a deadly affair. Maybe the Creator already has 1-3 cases in mind, but he'll need a lot more for an on-going series.

Hire a Researcher

Obviously, the Creator can do his own research, but if the Creator's a former tire shop owner, he/she may not have the know-how it takes to explore the subject matter in depth and find all the required information. However, a researcher is specially trained to dig deep and find the details that will make up each case each week.

One Show = One Case

For simplicity purposes, I recommend having each episode explore only one case or unsolved mystery. That will mean having to fill-up a one-hour slot, so the more case information's acquired, the more a Creator can be assured he's putting together a solid, factual show while exploring the show's potential for suspense.

Investigative Facts Aren't Entertainment

A novice mistake I often see is a Creator who believes the facts he's compiled are interesting enough to become a reality-TV show. Case in point, a Creator wants to investigate lost/stolen animals in a metropolitan area. Most audiences care about animals, but the Creator will need to dig deep into the pet's background for the touching story that will entertain the audience and keep them faithfully watching the show week after week.

In the series *My Cat From Hell*, the show's lead, Jackson Galaxy, is entertaining with his tattoos, love of music and a guitar case filled with animal toys and kitty treats. Weekly, he explores why a cat's misbehaving and helps correct the problem. This entails digging deep into the cats past behavior and learning the pet's background.

It's these personal cat stories combined with the intriguing character/host that keeps the audience coming back week after week. The show goes beyond the mere facts of what's causing the cat's bad behavior and gives us a personal, insider's look into the world of cat owners and their feline pets.

By the way, notice how the *My Cat From Hell* creates suspense and goes beyond simply conveying information. In each episode, Jackson must fix the cat's issue or the pet could face rehoming, being returned to a kennel or worse. This creates tremendous suspense and asks the question, 'Will Jackson be able to fix the kitty and maintain peace and harmony in the household he's helping? Or will the kitty lose its home?

Remember, regardless of the investigative series you've chosen, suspense is key. If the subject matter is interesting, but it lacks suspense, start asking questions and coming up with ways to layer suspense into the series. Without suspense, a manual's been created rather than an Investigative Series.

Break into 4-Segments

If a Creator is new to reality-TV or writing/creating in general, he may not know for sure if he has enough material to sustain a series let alone a single episode. Don't worry about the entire series for now, focus on one episode and break it up into segments to determine if there's enough viable information, suspense and entertainment for the episode. The investigative series requires a one-hour format, with approximately 4 segments that run 10-12 minutes each (minus commercial breaks).

Most shows have commercial breaks. There are usually 4 to 5 commercial breaks per show. Let's look at how *My Cat From Hell* sets up the segments as an example. In the first segment, before the first commercial break, we meet Jackson and his clients, the cat and its family and get an overview of the problem. Right before the commercial break hook the audience so they won't turn the channel.

In *My Cat From Hell*, this 'hook' usually comes right after Jackson asks what happens if the problem can't be resolved and we discover the cat will be rehomed. Suddenly, the show goes to commercial break and we're left hanging wondering what will happen next.

In the second segment, Jackson gives the client homework and options for resolving the issue and has the cat owner videotape the pet's progress. This is factual information that the Creator has to keep entertaining. This is accomplished by revealing the downside of what part of the cat's rehabilitation isn't working. Often the pet isn't responding as anticipated and other things must be tried. This builds suspense as the audience wonders if the pet can be helped or will have to be rehomed. End this segment with the audience wondering if the pet can be helped or not.

In the third segment, things are starting to look up, but there's usually one thing still standing in the way of finalizing the deal. Maybe the cat is going in its liter box, but still likes to pee on the couch. Again, we're held in suspense. Can Jackson fix the problem in time or will dire measures happen to the cat?

Finally, in segment four (last part of the show before it ends), Jackson fixes the issue at the last possible moment and saves the day. Each show is handled in this same way to heighten the outcome, make it entertaining to watch and it creates a built-in suspense factor, which are all requirements to sell and sustain this type of investigative series.

Going beyond mere facts is imperative to selling this type of series, so take a good, hard look at the series you've created. Can it be segmented to be entertaining and create suspense that goes beyond just providing information? If the answer is YES, then the Creator is on his way to a viable, market ready reality-TV show.

Sidebar Interviews

Most investigative series, especially those involving crimes and mysteries, rely heavily on interviews obtained from authors and professionals in the show's field. Once the show is purchased, a producer will handle setting up these interviews, but in the creation process, the show's Creator may want to arrange several camera interviews to be used in a trailer, sizzle reel or even for an introductory pilot to be shown on a YouTube Channel (more on this later).

I've personally found that in most cases people will speak with you, but only if the Creator appears to have the necessary credentials to warrant the time of a police chief or a famous author. If the Creator is just starting out, he/she may have to rely on the desk clerk at a police station for a quick interview or the author's assistant before moving up to the big leagues. Get whatever you can on camera. Less isn't more in reality-TV. More is more!

Beta Test the Investigative Series

I've mentioned Beta Testing for other series and it's vital at this early stage to determine if the Creator has a strong enough show to compete in the reality-TV market. It's also wise to consider the fact that producers will test audience the show and the Creator doesn't want any surprises. It's best to find out now what does and doesn't work and fix it accordingly rather than have a producer turn down the show because it's lacking in one area or another. The Creator will only get one shot at Hollywood. Don't blow it!

For this type of series, have a questionnaire prepared ahead of time with tough questions. Ask things like:

– What did you find suspenseful about the show?
– Did you find the show entertaining? If not, why?
– What did you like about the show?
– What did you dislike about the show?
– Would you tell your friends/family about the show?
– Was the show's information presented in an entertaining way?

- On a scale of 1-10, with 10 being the best rating, how would you rate this show?
- If you could change something about the show, what would it be?
- Would you watch this show weekly and/or set a DVR to record it weekly?
- Is there a similar show you like better than this show? If so, why?
- Is the title catchy and memorable?
- Do you like the key characters in the show? (If the show doesn't have a key character, does the audience like how the characters are presented?)
- Do you have any comments or questions?

Have the test audience watch the series without any verbal introduction from you, the Creator. Ask them to fill out the questionnaire during the show and/or they can complete it after the show. Collect the questionnaires and compare results. Fix areas where more than one beta tester mentioned the same problem. The rest is subjective and should be treated as such.

Be careful here. I've seen Creators do this only to ignore the audience's comments and concerns. The Creator needs to set aside his/her ego and make the necessary changes to assure the series has the best chance at being picked up by a network.

Keep the Results

Always keep the results of the Beta Test even after fixing any problem areas. This information can be used later or even for creating a secondary, spin-off show or a new, original series.

Quick Overview

- Creating Suspense is Key
- Inconclusive Show Endings Require Suspense

- Elusive Subject Matters Require Special Handling
- Determine if the Concept is Interesting & Entertaining
- Consider Hiring a Researcher
- Investigative Facts must be Entertaining
- Break the show into 4-Segments
- Obtain Sidebar Interviews
- Beta Test the Investigative Series
- Keep the Results

✤ CREATE THE PARANORMAL SERIES

The paranormal series is by far one of the most popular and sought-after reality-TV shows on the market today. Audiences can't get enough and the suspense factor is built-in because an apparition could appear at anytime. The Creator doesn't even have to layer in suspense because it's built into the concept. The Creator often doesn't have to rely on experts for sidebar interviews, like in other series, because the team that hosts the show provides the necessary interviews that fills the airtime and/or those experiencing the paranormal activity can be interviewed.

While the show is easier to put together than other series with more demanding content, there are drawbacks to the paranormal series that the Creator should consider.

The Saturated Paranormal Market

There are a lot of paranormal shows on the air and hundreds (maybe thousands) more being marketed to Hollywood daily. But don't despair. This chapter is going to help the Creator put together a competitive package.

There are two factors to consider when it comes to beating out the competition. The most important is the SPIN FACTOR and secondly is the TEAM DYNAMICS. Let's take a look at each.

First, be aware that paranormal shows that are being turned down do NOT have a spin factor and the Creator did NOT consider the Team Dynamics. Ignoring or missing one or both of these factors will sink a show fast.

The Spin Factor

The Spin Factor is simply a unique or original approach to the concept of investigating the paranormal world. The success of the hit paranormal series like *The Dead Files* relies on the spin factor. In this series, the paranormal isn't investigated by a normal team, but rather by a psychic medium and a retired homicide detective. They don't compare notes until the end of the show, which creates a dual-layer of suspense as we wonder if they came up with the same information. It has a double suspense factor, a unique presentation of the findings and a unique approach to the subject matter.

Be careful here. Many Creators will think they have one unique factor and it's enough to sell the show, but is it? For example, I know a team who acquired exclusive rights to film in a remote, abandoned asylum and thought this would be enough to give their show the spin factor it would need to sell.

Wrong! Having a unique location is cool, but the producers considering this show quickly realized the audience would get bored with watching the same location week after week. And this is a huge location that could have been broken up into weekly segments, but it wasn't enough SPIN to sell the series.

Could the Creator turn this around somehow? Yes, in fact, I suggested the Creator use the asylum as a home base for the team (that's unique), update the audience on new activity at this location weekly, but go out and investigate other asylums and literally become the *Asylum Hunters*. No, this isn't the title of their show, but I'm using it as an example of how to take a lackluster approach to the SPIN and beef it up enough to gain the attention of Hollywood producers.

The SPIN can come in a variety of forms. Here are some examples of how to mix and match SPIN FACTORS to create a viably strong market contender in the paranormal series field:

- Unique location(s)
- Expert Team Members
- Unique Way of Investigating
- Unique Way of Presenting the Evidence
- Any combination of the above

Team Dynamics

I had a client who had a really unique spin to his paranormal series and I was anxious to watch the sizzle reel he'd put together for it. Upon watching it, my heart sank. The team he'd put together were high school buddies who were as nerdy as they come and spoke like NASA scientists to the point I couldn't understand what they were talking about.

The team dynamics sunk the series. Watching paint dry would have been more interesting. In fact, two of the guys were clearly uncomfortable being in front of the camera and that even made things worse.

In real life, these guys were bosom buddies, but their friendship just didn't translate into a sellable product. We've all met people we have common interests with and who become lifelong friends, but for a series like this, the Creator needed to look for CHEMISTRY!

You know those people, whether their two buddies who act like brothers or former co-workers who can finish each other's sentences or are so diversely different that they automatically create a dynamic effect! In the long-running paranormal series *Ghost Adventures*, the team dynamics of Zak Bagans and his buddies speaks for itself and is a major selling factor.

This doesn't mean the team members need to know each other. The Creator might know an eccentric psychic and team him or her up with a paranormal non-believer who the Creator found via interviews. Coming up with this Chemistry is key to selling a paranormal series.

What if the Creator's not sure about the chemistry? Then videotape the team together in action. Go out on a ghost hunt then play back the tape when the team is absent. Really watch and scrutinize if the dynamics work or not, and be prepared to make tough changes before coming up with a team dynamic that will sell. *Ghost Hunters* underwent some vital team changes that kept the series alive and were smart to do so. Unfortunately, in today's competitive market, the Creator of a paranormal show no longer has the luxury of waiting until the series hits the air to determine if the team dynamics work or not. The Creator will need to make the tough changes and decisions up front before proceeding to market.

As part of the team dynamics, the Creator will need to determine how many will be on the team and that means how many actually appear on camera and in every show weekly. In *The Dead Files*, there are three main team members that appear weekly. There are also three main team members in *Ghost Adventures*, while other shows have more or less. It's the chemistry and dynamics between the team members that counts.

Note: This type of show isn't as likely to work with one person. Why? Because part of the built-in suspense of ghost hunting is watching the reaction between the team members when they make a discovery and that requires more than one person in front of the camera.

Technology and/or Experts

Paranormal series rely on one of two key factors. The show must relay on high-end technology, like infrared-red cameras and audio recording devices, and/or experts, like psychics, priests, demonologists, etc., for the show to have credibility with the audience.

Without one of these two factors, the show will appear amateurish to the audience. This can be tough on the Creator who is trying to put together a series on a limited or non-existent budget.

As for equipment, the Creator can start off small with a few pieces picked up on Ebay, rented for a few days or even borrowed. Borrowing might seem out of the question, but a smart Creator will invite the equipment's owner along on the ghost hunt to participate in the moment and to have someone on hand who knows how things works. And who knows, this person could become a dynamic team member!

Experts can be more difficult to pin down than equipment, especially if the Creator wants to use the experts as a regular on the show. Putting up notices or adverting at local colleges for experts in the paranormal field or similar fields is probably the easiest approach since the Creator will know the party contacting him/her is already interested.

The Creator might have to do some calls and leg work in person for other experts, like priests, demonologists, etc., who may be more reluctant to become involved, especially when it means appearing on camera. The reasons vary from not wanting to look foolish to receiving scrutiny from their colleagues. I think this is why more and more shows that do make it on the air seem to rely more on tech guru types who are used to cameras and don't care who scrutinizes them. In fact, they can use it to promote themselves in their future endeavors.

Personally, I'd love to watch three old priests hunting demons, but getting that group together might not be realistic. However, if a Creator can pull off this type of awesome dynamic, he has a winning reality-TV show on his hands.

One extra note: Speaking of 'old' experts, one way to potentially get the experts required for a paranormal show is to seek out retired experts or those who no longer work in that particular field, but still have the know how. The show *Fact, Faked or Paranormal* is hosted by former FBI agent Ben Hansen who leads his team on investigations to determine if incidents, mostly derived from video content, are real or faked. Ben's not a paranormal expert, but he is an investigative expert, which makes him the perfect individual to recruit for a paranormal series.

Most of us know former cops, federal agents, military personnel, professors, business owners, people with specialized skills, etc., who might make exceptional experts to recruit for a show. I wouldn't advise approaching this person directly, but rather gauging their interest in the subject matter first. One way is to invite them on a preliminary ghost hunt and gauge their response. Did they love it? Could they go every night if invited? Did they enthusiastically tell everyone about the experience? If so, you have the perfect person to approach for the series. Get them red hot for the concept before hitting them with a sales pitch to become an on-camera team member. The Creator has a much better chance at scoring a long-term team member this way.

What about the Creator? Many paranormal shows are hosted by their own Creator and rightfully so. Who knows more about the subject matter than the person who put it all together! This person most likely already has the dynamic team factor required to make it all happen. Don't be shy! Consider getting in front of the camera. You only live once! Go for it! In fact, in the show *Ghost Adventures*, the 3-guy team films each other with handheld cameras. That's a unique approach to getting in front of the camera. And the show's Creator, Zak, is the host.

The Show's Format

A paranormal series works best in a one-hour format, but that's a lot of time to fill and just watching a team walking around a building with equipment can get boring fast.

However, I don't think the Creator needs to worry about this so much in the creation stage (other than determining if the Creator has enough content for the time frame) because once the show airs, it'll come down to creative film editing. But for the purpose of presenting a presentation to the industry, the Creator will need to go on those long, overnight hunts and risk capturing nothing at all or maybe a quick 5-second haunting moan that sets the stage for the show. Use whatever evidence is collected for the trailer, sizzle reel of pilot episode.

If the Creator decides to film the pilot episode, then break up the slower moving parts with sidebar interviews, cut away to a central location that acts as a techno base where everything monitored, switch back-n-forth between team members, and ease into the big moments and milk them for what they're worth.

Expert Advice Instead of a Beta Test Audience

For almost every other type of series, I advocate running the trailer, sizzle reel or pilot episode through a beta test audience, but that won't work for this type of series. Why? Because everyone likes paranormal and it takes the trained, expert eye to determine from a 1-minute trailer, a 10-minute sizzle reel or the pilot episode, whether the team has the dynamics and the show is unique enough to warrant a time slot on the networks or cable TV.

Look up services that provide screenplay/TV pilot coverage and ask them if they'd critique the concept and whatever else you have, like a trailer, sizzle reel and/or pilot episode. Present it to this party like you'd present it to a Hollywood producer. Yes, you'll have to pay for this critique, probably anywhere from $99 to a couple hundred, but it'll be worth it. Feel free to give them your questionnaire, in addition to receiving their critique.

Quick Overview

- Understand how to Compete in the Saturated Market
- The Spin Factor
- Team Dynamics

- Decide if the show relies more on Technology or Experts
- Get Expert Advice Instead of a Beta Test Audience

If the Creator is working with a $0 budget, then ask the industry coverage expert to give a review in exchange for a credit on the PILOT EPISODE ONLY. The credit should be CONSULTANT and give them a contract that says they get this credit. Only do this with one party. The Creator doesn't want to have a list of 50 consultants to add to the credits. Make sure the consultant understands this is a speculative reality-TV presentation that may or may not get on the air.

✥ CREATE THE MONSTER SERIES

Is the Monster Audience Friendly?

Is the audience familiar with the monster? We've all heard of the Loch Ness Monster often referred to as Nessie and entire series could be built around such a well-known monster, but the subject's been done a lot in documentaries. Instead, you might opt to go with a lesser-known lake monster, like Champ, the Lake Champlain monster. But would a Creator have enough material to sustain a series with the lesser-known monster and would the audience be as interested in this monster as they are in the Loch Ness monster?

Lesser-known monsters might be tougher to sell, like the Jersey Devil, the Chupacabra, etc., for several reasons:

- Don't have the wide audience appeal of the other monsters.
- Very little material about these monsters to sustain a series.
- Lack of experts who can speak regarding the probability of the monster's existence.

Location Consideration

It might sound fascinating to hunt the Abdominal Snowman and documentaries have been made about this creature and/or its rare sightings have been the subplots of episodes of *Finding Big Foot*, but sustaining a team under harsh winter conditions for months on end is a very expensive endeavor and most shows simply don't have the budget to cut it. Besides, who wants to live on an icy mountain for seasons at a time?

Monsters that live in remote places, like an icy tundra, jungles, deep sea, etc., can be the most difficult to create an on-going series around and are usually the subject of documentaries or are mentioned along with other monsters in related shows.

Expert Considerations

As I noted above, finding experts for lesser-known monsters can be difficult. The Creator will be lucky to find witnesses and is more likely to deal with historians or local elders who've heard legends, but few have ever seen the monster.

This can cause a problem in the form of a lack of experts to do interviews for the series. Believe it or not, there are experts in the field of Big Foot who've spent years documenting, searching for and speaking about the monster, but few such experts for monsters like the Jersey Devil or the elusive Chupacabra.

An ALL-IN Monster Series

Perhaps you've decided to do a series about ALL the monsters out there, making each episode about a different monster. That has been done and it's still doable, but the Creator will have to give it a spin. Perhaps the team is lead by a retired zoologist or a former big game hunter or a concept that gives the show a unique spin.

I'd advocate against all-monster series unless the team leader is somehow unique, like Josh Gates of *Destination Truth* and *Expedition Unknown*. He's a unique personality with a degree in archaeology and drama, and he's traveled to over 50 countries. Audiences seem more drawn to shows that zero in on one particular monster rather than globe hopping. However, if you truly believe you have a unique approach to the monster series, like a dynamic team leader, then go for it.

Some Creators might decide to worry 'bout the experts after they've sold the show and go with a one-sheet only (we'll discuss this later), but I'd advise the Creator to do the homework and find out if there are viable experts in the field who can be called upon for interviews. If there are only 2 Chupacabra experts in the world and neither one wants to appear in the series, then the Creator's show could tank before it even gets on the air.

Does the Series Hold Suspense?

Like the Investigative Series, the Monster Series must hold the audience in suspense even if the subject matter is a well-known monster. This can be tricky because Creators often tend to inundate the audience with interesting facts believing this is enough to hold the audience's interest, but it isn't. The audience isn't watching the show to be fed a textbook of 'interesting' facts. They want to be entertained.

In the Investigative Series, it's easy because the Creator can withhold information until late in an episode and create suspense. Considering the monster isn't likely to be found, there's no information to hold until later. Instead, the Creator will need to improvise. Watch the *Finding Big Foot* show as an example of how to do this. They'll gather witnesses and map out locations to go on a night hunt. The anticipation of the night hunt creates suspense. Will they have a sighting or encounter the creature like the witnesses did? What will happen? The Creator always wants to go to 'hot spots' where the elusive creature has been seen, is said live or frequent. Even if there are no recent eyewitness accounts, the Creator can still sustain the suspense by hyping up the fact that if there's going to have an encounter with the monster that this would be the place.

One Hour or 30-Minute Format?

Most monster series are one-hour formats, but if the Creator's diving into the world of a lesser-known monster, a 30-minute series might be more engaging and work better for attention deficit audiences.

The trick here is to start off the pilot with a bang! Go for the biggest sighting possible and investigate it. Really lock the audience into the possibility that this lesser-known monster might really be out there.

Beta Test the Series

Whether the Creator's done a one-sheet, a trailer, a sizzle reel or has filmed the pilot episode, I'd recommend running the concept through a test audience. This can be exceptionally helpful with lesser-known monsters that may or may not spark an audience's interest. It won't take long for the Creator to know if he has a hit series or a big, fat flop.

Keep the Results

Always keep the results of the Beta Test even after fixing any problem areas. This information can be used later or even for creating a secondary, spin-off show or a new, original series.

Quick Overview

- Is the monster audience friendly?
- Location Considerations
- Expert Considerations
- An ALL-IN Monster Series
- One Hour or 30-minute Format
- Does the Series Hold Suspense?
- Beta Test the Series
- Keep the Results

✧ CREATE THE INFORMATION SERIES

This type of series may seem to encompass many of the others already outlined, but it is different because it usually doesn't involve teams or hold suspense. It's shows like *Through the Wormhole* or *The Story of God*, both narrated and hosted by actor Morgan Freeman.

These shows are usually hosted by and/or narrated by a celebrity or a field expert. They demand a high profile or dynamic lead to carry the series. They can also be a more difficult series to maintain (and sell) because there's a lot of interesting information, but the show rarely holds any suspense.

Pay Special Attention to the Subject Matter

These types of shows require the Creator to pay special attention to the subject matter. In fact, I'd recommend the Creator research the audience first to determine if there is an audience for their chosen subject matter and if that audience can stick around long enough to make the series successful.

The subject matter of the two shows hosted by Freeman is science and religion. Both handle vague subjects and while they hold a wide audience appeal, the content of the show's individual episodes may not be enough to sustain an entire series.

For example, let's say the Creator wants to do a show on Dark Matter, the elusive energy source in the universe that scientists are just beginning to understand. There are plenty of experts in the field, machines have been built to detect it and entire basement stations have been constructed to capture and record it.

However, after an episode or two, an audience could grow tired of the subject matter and the series will flop. Take a good, hard look at the information series you've chosen.

Why do *Through the Wormhole* and *The Story of God* resonate with an audience more than a series about Dark Matter? I believe it's because they speak to human nature and create a divine understanding of who we are, why we're here and what happens to us after death. It's this quest for answers to the core of human questions that keeps the series interesting, but not enough is known about Dark Matter yet to determine if it fits this criteria.

Beta Test the Series BEFORE Starting

For most series, I've recommended Beta testing after the Creator has the series packaged and wants to determine if it's lacking in any way that could cause it to be rejected by show runners. This will allow time to make changes before proceeding to market.

However, with the Information Series, it's best to test the market to determine if there is a sustainable audience for the subject matter BEFORE starting.

It might also be wise to steer away from taboo subject matters. Although they might seem interesting and even hold stories of human nature, audiences simply don't want to see them. They range in subjects from animal cruelty to the medical profession. Yes, animal shows can be huge and there's an entire channel, Animal Planet, dedicated to such shows, but a Creator can cross the line if he wants to do a show about a kill shelter. Who wants to become attached to a loving cat or dog only to discover no one ever adopted the pet and it was euthanized? The medical professional contains something most people don't want to see on TV, real blood. Fake blood and a gory scene once in the while from the news is the limit for most audiences.

However, there are medical-related reality TV shows dealing with real-life coroners, but it's rare we go inside a hospital, hospice, etc. If you've decided on this subject matter for a show, really do the homework to make sure it has a sustainable audience.

A clue to a taboo subject is if the Creator's never seen the subject done before in a reality-TV format or a documentary series. There isn't a series about rape victims for a reason. While the subject may become part of another on-going series, like the Investigative Series, it's unlikely to become a series onto itself.

Team, Field Expert or a Celebrity

The next consideration after the subject matter is how the show's presented. These types of shows rarely have teams because there simply isn't enough to investigate or explore that would justify the involvement of an entire team.

A field expert could work if it's someone who's dynamic in front of the camera. Do they have a personality an audience likes or are they nerdy, scientific and perhaps a bit flat on camera? A quick on-camera interview could help make this determination. Or the Creator might be able to recognize the unique, quirky, dynamic personality without the interview because the individual stands out in his or her field. Is this person interested in being part of a series that could run for months or even years?

Lastly, the celebrity host and/or narrator might actually be easier to find, locate and secure for a series than the field expert because celebrities are used to being in front of the camera and are often seeking new projects to become part of. There are two approaches to finding a celebrity for the series:

1. Find a celebrity that fits the series, like Morgan Freeman who seems ideal for *The Story of God* as a senior facing mortality, the audience can relate to him and his deep-set voice resonates with audiences.

2. Find a celebrity who's never done something like this before, but wants to remake their image, like the *Vanilla Ice Project* where the rapper turned house flipper provides a fresh spin on the subject matter.

I'm sure most of you are wondering how you'd approach a celebrity with a pitch for a series. The best way is to have at least a basic presentation of what the series is about, how it's laid out, format, audience, etc. If possible, provide something visual, like a quick trailer to 'tease' them to become interested.

The celebrities who'll be most receptive to doing a series are ones with their own production companies where they can literally become part of the production process. Others with agents or managers may be more difficult to approach because their representative(s) may not be accepting unsolicited material.

How do Creators find celebrities with their own production companies? Subscribe to IMDB Pro, which will give the Creator access to the celebrities entire profile, including any affiliated production companies, plus the company's name, address, phone, fax and email. Write a strong, one-page query letter and send to the celebrity. Go beyond telling them about the series and really sell them on the idea.

Slant it toward what the series can do for the celebrity. Can it fulfill a dream of exploring or going on an adventure, representing a subject matter, hunting a monster, participating in a game or paranormal activity they are personally interested in? Can the show become a vehicle for a comeback to the entertainment industry, perhaps after a long absence? Can it give the celebrity the opportunity to show diversity by doing something outside the box?

Don't ask the celebrity these questions. Do your homework. Study their career, interests, background and read any interviews that might give the Creator a clue as to what might intrigue the celebrity enough to sign on with the series. The reasons for doing a reality-TV show are usually more personal-based for a celebrity than doing a feature film or a regular TV show. They usually have a personal reason for being involved with the show. An example is Steven Seagal's series *Lawman* where we meet Steven, the fully commissioned deputy on duty in Louisiana. Few would have known he's a deputy without this series and he only did the series because he's personally committed to law enforcement.

Look for celebrity traits, talents, skills, hobbies, etc., that may not be known to the public, like Steven's work with law enforcement. Who knows, the Creator might discover that a celebrity once trained to be an astronaut or another celebrity treks the world creating unique food dishes. Any of these areas could be used to approach the celebrity and the Creator could land a solid series with a built-in audience who already know and like (or even dislike) the celebrity. Having a celebrity attachment to a project is a win/win situation that could quickly propel the series to a top spot on network or cable TV.

Finally, the added bonus of having a celebrity on board is that almost any subject matter, with the exception of taboo subjects, can quickly become entertaining masterpieces.

Extra Note: The celebrity should NOT be considered a funding source. The Creator should take the project to a show runner (TV producer) for funding and studio backing and/or find private funding. The exception is if the celebrity wants to become a producer on the show and/or fund the show. That's fine, but he/she should suggest it.

✣ CHARACTER DRIVEN VERSUS CONCEPT DRIVEN SERIES

There are other types of series that overlap with the types of series already mentioned and they include character driven and concept driven series.

CHARACTER DRIVEN SERIES

A character-driven series like *Little Women of L.A.* is 100% about the characters and usually involves a number of characters rather than a focal point character, celebrity or field expert. Suspense is usually replaced by the day-to-day drama that takes place in the lives of the series' characters.

Series Requires a Unique World

The twist a Creator will need to sell this type of series is interesting characters in a unique world. Most of us have never experienced what it's like to live the life of the rich and famous in Beverly Hills. This world intrigues an audience who'll return week after week to watch *The Real Housewives of Beverly Hills* verbally fight it out. It's primetime drama for real!

Most of us have never met a 'little person' and experiencing life from their perspective makes the entire world a unique place and it causes audiences to watch and become engaged in shows like *Little Women of L.A.* and *Big People, Little World.*

Suspense's Replaced by Drama

These types of series are put together with a group of individual stars, which can make the series harder to present to a show runner. If even one of the stars decides to drop out of the series, it can create an issue. The up side is that the Creator can easily replace a character without sacrificing the entire series. The series can go on for season after season with the same of even different characters, which is often the case with a drama-based series.

Drama is King

The character driven series relies on weekly drama between the stars to keep the audience coming back. If everyone's getting along in the sewing circle, the show will fail, but if Sue Ellen is plotting to get Cathy kicked out, then the series holds drama that the Creator can milk week after week to create drama and hold the audience in suspense.

Downside to a Character Driven Series

Hate to say it, but there are downsides to trying to maintain and sustain a series like this and they are as follows:

1. The cast usually contains drama kings and queens who will not only pick a fight with each other, but with you! They might want unrealistic perks, like special water for their hair or a chef for their cat. The easiest way to avoid these issues is to make it clear – IN WRITING – the rules and regulations for being on the show and stick with them. No exceptions! Get this contract signed BEFORE day one of filming.

2. Creators of these shows often have to film hundreds of hours of footage to get enough material for a single episode. The sewing circle dispute could run for several weeks, but only provide enough material for a one show. The Creator will have to make the tough decisions as to whether the series can be carried on past a few episodes.

3. The Creator knows a group of people and they present a unique world for the audience, but they all get along. There's no drama! No matter how unique the group, the series won't sell without drama. The characters don't have to be strangling each other; even a subtle disagreement among brothers can create drama and keep a series alive. A clever Creator will find these 'drama' spots and exploit them for the series.

4. A mutiny takes down the ship! Something happens that pisses off the entire cast. Maybe a rumor starts that one cast member is making more than someone else. True or not, the entire cast quits! It's actually more likely to happen with a larger, character driven cast, then a smaller team or with a lead star.

5. Might be harder to put together a character driven series from an idea only. Maybe the Creator has the idea to do a series 'bout Gold Miners in Alaska, but they're reluctant to come aboard because of environmental consequences that could be faced by exposing their day-to-day operations to a reality-TV show. This type of series has the best chance if the Creator knows a group of individuals up front and can work with them to bring the series to the networks and/or cable TV.

6. Greed, greed and greed! It's a huge misconception that anything related to Hollywood must have oodles of money attached to it. Individuals in the cast or the entire cast may have unrealistic expectations 'bout the salaries they'd receive by being regulars on the show. Before making a proposal to the cast, speak with a representative from the Screen Actors Guild (Yes, they handle reality-TV cast members too) and get some solid figures of realistic pay rates and present the

'minimum' number to the potential cast member(s). Show them SAG's minimum chart and stick with those rates to avoid salary disputes.

7. Faking Reality-TV! There may come a time in the show when the disputes become boring, repetitive and lack drama. The Creator may need to bring in a ghostwriter to spruce things up a bit. Maybe add a few biting sidebars that keep the drama going or setup 'fake' real scenarios that present new drama for the cast members. In other words, the Creator has technically become a Director and is directing non-actors on how to 'act' like something is real.

CONCEPT DRIVEN SERIES

In my opinion, this is the hardest series type to sell because audiences usually prefer a specific character or characters to follow and have a vested interested in. One series that has successfully handled the concept driven premise *is Ice Road Truckers.*

One could argue that the series crosses lines with other series types noted above, but a unique aspect of this series is the ever-changing cast that's literally different every season. A trucker is willing to risk his life for high pay by driving a loaded semi of equipment over a frozen body of water during the winter months in the outback of Alaska. Men have literally lost their lives!

Frankly, if the Creator is just starting out in the business and/or doesn't have a track record, I'd steer clear of this type of series. It's okay to have a cool concept, but bring in the memorable characters, teams, experts, celebrities, etc., needed to lock in the audience.

Concept Must Have a New Spin

I've noted above that the series premise can be something that's already been done, but give it a new spin. This is especially important if the concept has already been done or there are currently similar shows on the air. A new spin can be an exotic location, a diverse team, a surprise celebrity, or a unique way of handling the material. If the concept's too much like a similar show, it'll be rejected.

Create Suspense

Like a new spin, the concept won't sell without suspense. Find the series type closest to your show's idea and read that section in this book to discover ways to create suspense within a series. Interesting information won't be enough. Suspense is key!

Bring in Memorable Characters

As noted earlier in this section, I'd advise bringing in a memorable cast. Creators who deal strictly in ideas should try the film business; TV is a talking heads medium where the characters are the stars more than the concept. This isn't always true, but it is 99% of the time when it comes to reality-TV shows.

Budget Considerations

As noted earlier in this book, TV shows have a limited budget compared to film and many show Creators prefer to Executive Produce their own shows (Executive Producer = Money Man). Either way, the budget should be kept to a minimum per episode. A show 'bout NASA won't cut it because the costs to insure the show alone would far exceed most Creator's budget limits.

Follow the Overlapping Rules

Most concept driven series will overlap with one of the other series types mentioned in this chapter. If so, read through that section and follow all the rules that apply to putting that type of series together for a Hollywood Pitch Package Presentation.

Final Word

It's important to understand what the Creator will need to gather in terms of content, materials, characters, etc., and put together a Hollywood Pitch Package Presentation to the entertainment industry BEFORE proceeding to market. Just winging it and hoping you can sell a show with a verbal pitch is fools gold. The smart Creator takes the time to carefully craft a series and knows all the show's logistics, which will help avoid problems later.

Being prepared also helps a Hollywood producer see the potential in the show and will help get the producer excited 'bout bringing the show to an audience. All a verbal pitch does is present more questions than answers, while a Hollywood Pitch Package Presentation answers all the questions and moves the producer to the point of being able to see the show in a solid, finalized format.

CHAPTER FOUR

PREPARE A PITCH PRESENTATION

❖ PUTTING TOGETHER A PITCH PACKAGE

The Creator has learned how to get things started, how to identify what type of series best fits a show and what goes into putting together the different types of series.

The Creator has compiled the show's information, what it's about, competition factors (if applicable), budget limitations, run time, interviews, trailers (if applicable), sizzle reels (if applicable), cast, and beta tested the show with an audience. It's now time to learn how to put all this information into a presentation package to present to a Hollywood producer.

Each Presentation Is Unique

Hollywood follows a set of rules regarding format for TV scripts, feature film scripts, etc. These rules are stringent and if broken often result in a NO SALE situation. However, a reality-TV show presentation pitch has more flexibility and different rules than other material in Hollywood.

First, if you're a screenwriter or TV writer, you probably won't believe that you should add pictures to your presentation because you've been told to never add anything fancy to a script, like notes, comments, photographs, fancy font, etc. That's true, but the reality-TV pitch presentation is its own creative endeavor that could include all of the above.

This doesn't mean to create a photo album. The presentation should be a fine balance between imperative information and intriguing visuals that help sell the show. Think of it along the lines of a PowerPoint Presentation and it needs to have a polished, professional look.

Presentation Length

This will vary based on the Creator's finances. A package put together with little or no funds might be 1-3 pages long, while a higher-budgeted package could go up to 20-pages long.

Don't worry about the length. More isn't necessarily a selling factor. It's about quality, not quantity. A single-page presentation with the word LOST in the center of the page might sell before a 20-page series pitch about life in a Siberian circus.

What matters in terms of length are finances – yes, but it's also about sitting down at a table and laying out all the pieces of the series and selecting what jumps out as selling points. If you were a show runner who'd never heard of the series before, what would entice you to buy it? Pull out those selling points and set them aside. These MUST be in the package. This doesn't mean the rest is optional because there are certain things all Hollywood producers want to see in a package to help them determine if it's worth their time and effort to help bring it in to the studios and find the show an audience.

Here are ALL the things that can go into a reality-TV Pitch Package Presentation and should be considered by the Creator:

❦ COVER

The COVER should look slick, like a Hollywood movie poster. It might have a solid background with the show's title and a tagline or a background picture, title and a tagline. Keep it simple, memorable and professional looking.

Tagline

A tagline is a quick phrase that hooks the producer into the show's overall concept and/or characters. For the series *Naked and Afraid*, the tagline might be:

One Naked Man
One Naked Woman
One Endless Jungle

Picture the cover with a top/centered title, a jungle photographic background featuring the naked, over-the-shoulder shots of a man and woman with the tagline anchored to the right of the cover. It's simple and reveals visually and in a few words what the entire series is about; the conflict, suspense, characters, and even hints at a potential run time and budget.

Give the COVER a lot of thought. Look at movie posters, go through several drafts and take your time. It's a vital first impression that could land a sale in a single page!

Let's talk logistics of how to put this together. This book will give an overview of how to put together the Hollywood Pitch Presentation Package based on budget considerations.

Regardless of budget, I'd recommend the Creator read through ALL the sections from No Budget to High Budget. Often a Creator reads something in the high budget section that he/she believes can be modified to fit a low-budget and vice versa. Knowing all the options out there gives the Creator more ammunition to work with.

Photography

Photos used as a background for the COVER is a nice touch, but the cover photo will need to be professional quality. All budget levels should consider using stock photography that the Creator can purchase via a license ranging from 99 cents + from stock footage websites like Pond5.com, GettyImages.com, ShutterFly.com, etc. These are professional photographs broken down into categories for easy searching. Since the Creator isn't using the photograph for monetary compensation, like the sale of a book, but rather for presentation purposes only, the license should be royalty free.

WORD OF WARNING: Those who don't want to spend any money, not even a dollar, might try to copy/paste images from the web to use. This is a copyright violation and can cost the Creator big time. It's not worth it and the images are rarely high quality enough to go into the presentation. Pay the buck!

If the Creator has a medium to high budget for photography, a photographer can be hired to shoot images from the actual location or take still shots of the cast or even a group photo of the cast to use for the poster, but this won't be cheap. Or, if the Creator has an eye for photography and an HD camera (or cell phone camera), this could be used to create a cover, but make sure it looks high quality! In the case of using homemade photos, it's recommended to use software to enhance the photos quality, like Adobe Photoshop.

If the Creator has a larger budget, then the Creator can pull still shots from the trailer or sizzle reel and use them to create a cover photographic image. This is a specialized skill that might require the Creator to hire a Film Editor to prepare, but it's well worth the money because the poster will match the trailer and have a professional, polished finished look.

Cover Font

DO NOT USE any font that you'd normally use in a letter or in daily use. Go to the web and search for MOVIE POSTER FONTS. Pick one you like. Some you can download for free, while others might require a minimal fee – pay it! It's worth it and the COVER font will make the show look like it's already on the air!

Cast, Characters & Celebrities

If the Creator's locked down the cast with contracts (to be discussed in upcoming chapters), then the Creator has the rights to use their image on the COVER. However, if the Creator has not locked down the show's players yet – which is often the case – then DO NOT use their image(s) on the COVER.

NO CELEBRITIES on the COVER unless the Creator has a signed LOI (Letter of Intent) from the celebrity or his/her representation to do the show. Many Creators will argue this point stating they need to put a celebrity's picture on the COVER or in the body of the presentation to properly represent the show.

All the Creator is actually doing is looking like an amateur in front of a producer! If the Creator's show idea involves a celebrity personality, but the Creator doesn't have him/her locked in yet, then just state in the presentation that the show would be hosted or a celebrity like (name the actor) would be casted, but without pictures! After all, do you even have the rights to use their image in your presentation? If the answer is NO, then don't do it. There are other, more creative ways to adequately pitch the series.

Stay Away From...

Blank, white backgrounds. Stick with bold, solid background colors for the COVER or a photo that encompasses the entire poster COVER.

Fluorescent or neon colored fonts! This isn't Vegas. Stick with solid, professional movie poster fonts in complimentary colors that go with the background. A dark brown twig color might compliment a solid beige background. Use your imagination.

Too much wording! The COVER should have a 1-3 word title, a 1-3 line tagline with a few words (see under TAGLINE). Keep it simple, neat and clean looking. Less is more on a reality-TV presentation COVER.

Creator Lacks Creativity

If the Creator is in panic mode and ready to throw in the towel because putting together the COVER seems too overwhelming, stop! It's not too late! Nobody said you have to do it. It's just a suggestion to save money. The no budget Creator can trade pizzas with high school kids and get them to put it together for you! The medium to high budget Creator can pick and choose from creative companies across the web that will put a slick COVER together for a fee.

✾ TABLE OF CONTENTS

A TOC (Table of Contents) is only a consideration if the presentation package goes over 3-pages. It isn't necessary for shorter presentations. Keep this page simple. It's suggested that the Creator use the same font as the COVER, only in different sizes. Having different fonts on every page distracts from the content.

Keep the background a solid color, but make it something other than white. It can match the COVER color or compliment it. The Creator wants each page of the package to look like it belongs in the overall presentation.

For the rest of the page, keep it simple & straightforward:

TABLE OF CONTENTS

This page should be self-explanatory and fit any budget. Note: Many pitch presentation do NOT have a TOC. It's up to the individual Creator.

❦ CONCEPT PAGE

A mandatory page in the presentation is the CONCEPT page. Here's where the Creator lays out the show's premise. This page tells the producer what kind of series type it is and how it'll be presented to the audience on a weekly basis. Refer to the information you've compiled on the show and highlight the show's selling points on this page.

Perhaps it's the Monster Series that gives the audience the chance to come along on an adventure while CAPTURING BIGFOOT. It'll run an hour and the guest(s) will join a professional team to set traps to capture the elusive creature.

Don't Get Too Detailed

Remember, less is more! The goal is to sell the concept, not to tell the concept. The days are gone where we went to a video store to pick up a movie, but I can still recall turning over the DVD to read the back to determine if I wanted to rent the title or not. The back of the DVD is referred to in Hollywood as a 'blurb' that sells the concept to the DVD's potential buyer (or renter).

The CONCEPT page should read like the DVD blurb and be a selling point for the show. If the Creator isn't sure how to do this, then dig through the garage and find those old DVDs. If they've long since been chucked in the garbage, then spend a Saturday morning browsing yard sales. They usually have a few to purchase to use as a reference point. Sometimes you can even find the old VHS tapes – they're a powerhouse of blurbs the Creator can use as 'how to' examples.

The Creator can also look up the 'blurb' on www.IMDB.com, but it often doesn't have the strong selling points of those old DVD blurbs. The blurb should only be a few paragraphs long. Give an overview of the show, but keep the details, like team bios, locations, etc., for other pages in the presentation.

Open With a Question

Another technique the Creator can use to peak the producer's interest in the series is to open with a question on the CONCEPT page. The question might be something like: WHAT WOULD HAPPEN IF A TEAM CATCHES BIGFOOT? Lead with the question to introduce the series.

Add the Title

This might seem obvious, but be sure to mention the series title in the premise paragraphs on the CONCEPT page. It's often forgotten, but the Creator wants to keep that title fresh in the producer's mind.

Season Premiere

This may not apply to all types of series, but if it does, be sure to mention in a paragraph or two what the Season Premiere will be about. For example, in the CAPTURING BIGFOOT series, the season premiere might find the team and an audience guest in Oregon hunting the elusive creator. While a game show might find 5 contestants competing for a Caribbean cruise and an investigative series might find a field expert searching for clues in a cold case homicide. All of this information was laid out and prepared earlier. The Creator should reference the prepared information to create the presentation and to assure crucial show details aren't left out.

Season Finale

Like the season premiere, the Creator may or may not know how it's going to end. In an investigative series, the Creator may know that the final show will take the audience on a whirlwind search for a serial killer across three states. While the CAPTURING BIGFOOT team and their audience guest fly to the Alps to hunt big-foot's cousin, the Yeti.

If the Creator knows the Season Finale, then add it to the CONCEPT page in a brief paragraph or two.

If the Creator isn't sure about the first and last shows in a season, then don't add this information to the CONCEPT page. However, be prepared to answer questions about where the Creator sees the series going because a producer will want to see the show has the potential for longevity.

🐦 FEATURE PAGE

The FEATURE page will be different for every Creator and every show. This page should highlight a major FEATURE of the show. Unlike the CONCEPT page that is mostly text selling the story's concept to the producer, this page highlights something special about the series. Here's a sample rundown of what should appear on the FEATURE page for each type of series:

THE GAME SHOW SERIES

This is the page where the Creator presents the rules, regulations, prizes and details of how the competition will play out. How a contestant wins and how a contestant is eliminated. How many contestants start the game and on what episode will the winner be selected.

This page tells us the logistics of the game. Be careful not to get too detail oriented and bore a producer with bogged down information that becomes confusing. Keep the rules simple and something an audience with a high school level education can comprehend.

THE DOCUMENTARY SERIES

Highlight a celebrity narrator on this page with his/her picture and bio. If the series doesn't have a narrator, then highlight the series main concept, like *Ancient Aliens* might show a pyramid with a UFO flying over it. This page can be text and/or visually presented. The goal is to highlight a main feature of the series.

THE INVESTIGATIVE SERIES

This is a good time to highlight pictures of investigators from the field mixed with a few crime scene-type photos. Or photos that feature what the series might look like on the air. Sprinkle the page with captioned pictures.

THE PARANORMAL SERIES

If the Creator has an original ghost picture, then this is the place to add it. Be careful. Do NOT highlight the team here. Do a separate page dedicated to the paranormal team with their bios and pictures. However, the Creator might want to highlight the team's leader on this page.

THE MONSTER SERIES

A few shadowy, elusive pictures of the monster would be perfect to highlight this page. Try to make the picture(s) recent and something an audience hasn't seen before. For example, everyone's seen the famous Loch Ness Monster's lake photograph, but what if the Creator finds a more recent 'head shot' of Nessie – perfect! Use this new picture to highlight the series. It'll give it a fresh spin.

THE INFORMATION SERIES

The Creator should do something a little different for this series. Perhaps a Q&A list centered down the page that highlights the type of information the series will deal with. Here's an example:

What day will they discover the clue?
The Season Finale answers this question.

Will the star find true love or ride off into the sunset alone?
We'll find out when John makes a surprise appearance.

Susan thinks she's pregnant, but is Bill the father?
Stay tuned to find out when Susan's test results
are revealed live!

The Creator can add a photo of two or leave the Q&A session on a solid, color backing for emphasis.

CHARACTER DRIVEN SERIES

If the series has a star, then this is the place to highlight the star and provide his or her bio and picture(s). Remember, this is the entertainment industry, so be sure what the Creator adds to this page sells the star to the producer.

In a CAPTURING BIGFOOT series, the star might be a former big game hunter from Kenya. Be sure to mention that fact on the FEATURE page and add highlighted text points:

CAN A BIG GAME HUNTER CATCH BIGFOOT?

HE'S CAUGHT LIONS, TIGERS and RHINOS, **but BIGFOOT**?

(Add a picture next to each caption)

Keep it interesting to read and always toss in questions and leave them unanswered! This creates intrigue in the mind of the producer and like the audience he/she will want to know what happens next.

CONCEPT DRIVEN SERIES

This one can be tricky because highlighting a CONCEPT DRIVEN SERIES might get too informative and won't present the type of intrigue required to sell the series.

Get creative here. If the Creator's selling a CONCEPT DRIVEN SERIES revolving around science's attempt to locate black holes on earth, then maybe go a bit over-the-top and show a picture of a black hole swallowing earth. This goes beyond the concept a bit, but it captures the imagination and creates questions the producer will want answered and could land the Creator a sale.

❦ CAST, HOST, CHARACTERS, TEAM, & BIOS PAGE

Next, it's time to prepare a CAST, HOST, CHARACTERS, TEAM, & BIOS page that features the main players the audience will see weekly.

A photograph is MANDATORY! Let the producer get a look at the host, the cast or the team. Let the producer immediately see the possibilities. Keep the bios short and localized to information that helps sell the show's premise.

Make sure the photographs are professional quality and reveal the person in a positive way that sells the show. For example, the Creator of an outdoor sports show would be wise to select an exterior picture of the hunter with a bow & arrow rather than a picture of him/her cooking in a kitchen.

However, for a cooking show, it would be imperative to show the HOST or TEAM in a kitchen setting.

Keep everything to one page! For larger TEAMS, this will mean getting tough with the editing. Keep bios short, pictures high quality. The bios should be focused on skills, trades and information imperative to the show and nothing else.

Think of this page as a SNEAK PEEK moment from the show itself and try to make everyone presented on this page intriguing and sellable to an audience.

THE STAR should NOT be on this page, but be on the FEATURE page. To tie the two pages together, the Creator might open the page with something like....

....The show's star will be joined by:

Extra Creative Note: Mix things up. Angle a few pictures and offset the text. Keep the producer's eye moving across the page. A pitch presentation with a unique visual landscape will help the producer see the show's potential.

❦ LOCATIONS PAGE

Regardless of the type of series, the Creator would be wise to include a LOCATIONS page or at the least add the information to the CONCEPT page.

Why is this vital? Producers try to guesstimate the cost of a show and one way they do so is to determine what locations the show will be shot at weekly. Will the show be shot at one location, like a game show's studio set? Or will the show travel across the globe in search of elusive creatures?

The LOCATIONS page will highlight the locations. If it's a game show set, then show a picture of a game show set. Obviously, this won't be the show's actual set, but just an example of what it might look like or a representation of the overall competition concept.

If it's a broader location-type series, like an investigative series, then use stock photos from sites like Pond5.com to show intriguing labs, police stations, etc. Don't get too elaborate or the producer might think the show's costs outweigh its benefits. Stick to 2-5 locations and try to feature main locations the Creator believes will be in many episodes, like a police station or crime lab.

This page consists mainly of location photographs from the Creator's own camera or stock photographs. But, it's recommended the Creator add tidbits from the show on this page. For example, a photograph of a police station might be highlighted with a caption that reads: THE STAR'S HEADQUARTERS! Or show a surveillance camera pointed at a lake with the caption: WATCH FOR NESSIE 24/7!

Think outside the box. Keep each page interesting and intriguing. Try to present information in new ways the audience hasn't seen before.

Finally, if there's something unique about the location that isn't widely known by the public, then highlight that fact on the LOCATIONS page. For example, is the forest where the team's hunting Bigfoot also the location of the world's largest and most dangerous tarantula? Then put a picture up of the tarantula and caption it with: WILL THE TEAM CATCH BIGFOOT OR BE CAUGHT IN A DEADLY WEB?

Make sure the 'unique' aspect of the location isn't just empty information. It should relate to the show, create suspense, intrigue or danger for the show (like the tarantula) and be relative to the episode(s). If the Rangers in a forest are the only ones in the country who wear purple pants, who cares? It's only relevant if Bigfoot likes purple!

A word about reality-TV sets. We've already talked about game show sets and putting up a facsimile of what the show's competition stage might look like, but many reality-TV shows rely on locations like the characters' houses, business locations, etc. This is fantastic because the producer will see these as 'free' locations, which is a bonus. The Creator just needs to make sure to secure location agreements for filming (we'll discuss this later).

❦ FORMAT PAGE

The FORMAT page tells the producer how the show will play out weekly. Is it a one-hour format broken into four Acts? Or a 30-minute show broken into two Acts?

Don't be intimidated by the Format. Shows do vary, but for the purpose of a reality-TV there are two types of formats the Creator will need to become familiar with:

30-Minute Reality-TV Show Format

This show is broken into Two Acts. They include Act I and Act II. Each Act runs roughly 12-15 minutes and is separated by a commercial break. A show may have more than one commercial break, especially as it nears the end of the show where 1 to 3 extra commercial breaks are snuck in to assure the show can pay all its bills.

COMMERCIAL BREAKS

The Creator needs to understand that a commercial break is more than an advertisement to sell the consumer-watching audience a product or service. The money spent on advertising is what pays for the show; everything from craft service (catering) to salaries, sets, travel expenses, equipment, crews, makeup, clothing, permits, etc.

The show MUST leave room for commercial breaks, which means a 30-minute reality-TV show's actual run time is closer to 22-minutes.

For the FORMAT PAGE, the producer wants the Creator to reveal how the show will appear in each Act I. This will vary depending on the show's layout. For example, in a game show, the contestants might compete in various categories and several might be eliminated by the first commercial break, then in Act II, the finalists will compete until a winner is selected.

The easiest way to determine what takes place in the Acts for your show is to watch a comparative show. How is it laid out? What happens in Act I and in Act II? Use it as a model to come up with your show's format.

Keep it simple. State in a few brief paragraphs what happens in each Act. That's all the Creator needs for the Format Page, but make it concise and visual so the producer can see what it's about and get excited by the concept and its possibilities as a reality-TV show.

There is one additional thing the Creator should be aware of. The Creator needs something new happening in Act II. Think of it as a spin point. For example, in Act I of a competition show, multiple players might compete in a verbal Q&A contest, but in Act II, it might be a physical confrontation or a test of brute force.

1-Hour Reality-TV Show Format

The second type of reality-TV show format is the 1-hour format. For the purpose of a reality-TV show presentation, the show will have four Acts. Yes, most 1-hour shows have more than 4 commercial breaks, but this is the norm.

Each Act is 12-15 minutes in length and should end with a cliffhanger moment or a spin point that leads the audience into the next Act.

Watch TV shows that are similar to your show and note what takes place in each Act. Use this as a model for creating your show's format. Here's an example from the TV show *Finding Bigfoot*. The show is a one-hour format with four Acts and sticks to a basic breakdown each week as follows:

ACT ONE
Preliminary & random nighttime investigations.

ACT TWO
Gather Bigfoot info from locals.
Decide where to focus the investigation.

ACT THREE
The team investigates a hot spot area.
Highlights two teams at different locations.

ACT FOUR
Solo investigation with one highlighted team member.
Final wrap.

The Creator can break down the show like I've done here, but I'd also advise writing up a few descriptions of each Act in a few paragraphs that paint a clear and concise picture of the show.

❦ WRAP PAGE

The WRAP page is used to build a bit of hype for the show and to provide information about the Creator. Yes, it's your page!

First, let's talk about the hype. Keep it to a few opening lines near the top of the page. Try something like:

JOIN "CHASING BIGFOOT" WEEKLY AND DON'T MISS THE MOMENT THE TEAM CATCHES THE WORLD'S MOST ELUSIVE CREATURE!

The show's brought to you by:

This is where the Creator's picture, bio and contact information appears. Don't be shy! You're not being asked to appear before the camera, but you will need to highlight yourself if you want to sell the show.

Start with a professional picture, preferably a headshot type photograph. If the series is a game show, seeing the Creator in a nice suit or business attire is a good look. If the series is a monster series, maybe a jungle background with a nice shirt and a big smile. Keep the pose show related, if possible. The Creator wants to look like he or she is part of the show and capable of handling every aspect of its creation and execution.

Next, prepare a professional bio for the Creator. Start with any skill, trade or background that's even remotely related to the series. If you're a former cop, then state the Creator's a former LAPD officer turned Loch Ness Monster Hunter! If the Creator has a BA in Biology and has created a food competition show, the degree probably isn't relevant, but still mention it in a creative way:

> *While the Creator studied for his BA in Biology at Columbia, he created three famous macaroni dishes that'll be featured on the show and used in the final competition phase.*

Finally, add why the Creator has an interest in this show and how it is vital. The information might be a natural part of the bio, like a former cop who came up with a new angle on an investigative series. If not, then take the time to incorporate the information into the WRAP page.

Don't forget to include vital contact information; Creator's address, cell phone #, email, Facebook, Twitter and anything else that will allow the producer easy access to the Creator to make an offer for the project!

Extra Tidbit: Adding a 'thank you for taking time from your busy schedule to consider this project' is always a nice touch! It shows you appreciate the opportunity to present the series and you're professional in your approach.

How Many Pages for Each Section?

I'd advise one-page for each section noted above, but I have seen Creator's take 2-3 pages to introduce the cast, concept, etc. The rule = LESS IS MORE! It isn't about shoving information down the producer's throat. It's about selling him (or her) on a cool new TV show! Show and don't tell. Keep information brief, informative, visual and entertaining!

Overall Presentation

It should look slick, professional and I'd advise the Creator to make the final document an Adobe Acrobat .pdf file, which is most widely accepted by producers.

COPYRIGHT & WGA

Once the Creator has the reality-TV show package presentation in written form, it's time to copyright and submit the package to the WGA (Writer's Guild of America) to protect the creative concept from sticky fingers.

DO THIS BEFORE MARKETING!

For the U.S. Copyright office, go to www.copyright.gov. Costs vary. Check the website for updated information. Note: A copyright can take up to a year to obtain. The Creator only needs the Copyright's pending number, which is provided at the time of submitting the project.

For the WGA, go to www.wgaw.com. Scroll down on the right hand side to REGISTER SCRIPT here. Under this heading you'll find a place to register the presentation package (see Register a Treatment). Cost is $20.

✤ HOW TO PITCH THE SHOW VIA A PRESENTATION

The Creator has come up with an idea, determined the type of series and put together a reality-TV show pitch presentation. Now what?

It's time to pitch the show to Hollywood! This sounds like the hard part, but having a presentation will make it a lot easier to approach producers, actors and even private investors to get the show on the air. But wait a minute! You don't know anyone in Hollywood and have no idea where to start. This is true for the majority of reality-TV creators, but don't worry because you're going to learn where to start and how to get the presentation in front of Hollywood.

First, the Creator's marketing plan will depend on what type of package has been put together; No Budget Package, Low-Budget Package or a High-Budget Package. We'll discuss each package in detail in an upcoming chapter. Here's the basic breakdown:

Low-Budget Package
Consists of a written Presentation Package only.

Medium-Budget Package
Consists of a written Presentation Package.
1-3 minute trailer.

High-Budget Package
Consists of a written Presentation Package.
1-3 minute trailer AND a sizzle reel.
Potentially a YouTube Web Series.

Since most of you don't know someone in Hollywood to give the package to, start with what you do know, the INTERNET. Most of you are familiar with social media where there are many opportunities to network the project to an audience, like Facebook, Instagram, websites, etc.

QUICK JUMP START

A place to do a quick jumpstart that guarantees a producer's response is www.VirtualPitchFest.com. This site allows the Creator to pitch the project directly to Hollywood producers and agents/managers (they can rep the project and help market it). The purchaser of this service is guarantee a response from the producer within a certain period of time. In this business that's unheard of, so this makes this site an exceptional place to start.

However, the Creator won't be able to just send the presentation. The site requires a one-page query letter to the producer that pitches the project. WRITE IT NOW! Remember, the goal is to sell the project, not to tell us about the project. Go to your presentation package and pick out the selling points and make sure they're highlighted (even in BOLD) in the letter...something like THE SHOW THAT FINALLY FINDS BIGFOOT!

VERY IMPORTANT! The goal isn't to pitch the entire show via this query letter. Instead, the Creator's goal should be to get the presentation package into the producer's hands. That's the real selling point! After a brief, letter-style pitch, mention there's a pitch presentation package available and a trailer and/or sizzle reel for viewing. Most producers will take a peek even if the concept doesn't strike them at first and this is your chance to make the sale!

Don't be intimidated by the query letter pitch. If you're having a hard time writing the letter, the website has samples you can view and see how it's done.

The second website I'd recommend is www.TVWritersVault. com. A bit more expensive and there's no guarantee a producer will respond, but many network executives frequent the site browsing for new reality-TV concepts. For this one, you'll need to use parts of the presentation to submit (based on the sites rules/regulations) and be sure to mention if you have a trailer or sizzle reel.

The final site I'd recommend is www.InkTip.com. TV producers browse the site. Although they may say they have no interest in reality-TV, I guarantee if they run across a concept that intrigues them enough, they'll jump into the world or reality-TV. It has happened from this site and you could be next.

YOUTUBE

Next, if the Creator has a presentation package that includes a trailer and/or a sizzle reel (we'll discuss these later), then put it up on a freebie site like YouTube. DO NOT make it password protected. You want the world to see it and hope it goes viral!

Use the YouTube link to promote the show and send it out to anyone who wants to view it. The more likes you get the better.

Note: This is no substitute for the presentation package because the trailer and/or sizzle reel isn't going to cover vital information the producer wants to know, like the format, casting, sets, overall concept, etc. On the final frame of the YouTube video add a text note that states TO VIEW THE REALITY-TV SHOW PRESENTATION, CONTACT _____(add your name/email).

VERY IMPORTANT INFORMATION ABOUT YOUTUBE

This is probably the most important part of social media a Creator can use to sell a project because the Creator can track how many people have viewed the trailer and/or sizzle reel. If a Creator can show an interest in the trailer (or sizzle reel) of an audience of 200,000 or more, the Creator WILL GET THE ATTENTION of a Hollywood producer. There's nothing a producer loves more than buying a show with a built-in audience! MANY shows, like *Dead Files* have sold using this Internet marketing strategy.

This technique doesn't require the Creator to know anyone in Hollywood. In fact, Hollywood will most likely come to the Creator with a purchase offer! There's no other creative project in Hollywood that has this type of selling power at its fingertips.

FACEBOOK

Share trailers and/or sizzle reels on Facebook and ask your friend's list to share the video with others. Building hype for the project is vital to a sale.

The Creator may also want to consider starting a Facebook page for the project. Hype is the name of the game!

Build a Website

There are plenty of website companies that can help a Creator put together a professional looking website for the project. Make sure the website includes the presentation package and I'd advise asking the interested party to contact you via email for a password to view the presentation. That way you have a record of who has viewed the presentation. Obviously, add links to trailers and/or sizzle reels, Facebook pages, etc.

This is NOT MANDATORY, but any means used to spread the word about the project will be helpful.

Create a Blog

A blog is nothing more than an on-line diary where the Creator can present the project, update the audience on the status of the Project and build a daily, weekly or monthly record to show a producer that the show has an audience.

VERY IMPORTANT INFORMATION – AUDIENCE CREATION

The good news is that the Creator doesn't have to wait until the show airs to build an audience. In fact, building an audience while marketing is the #1 way to sell the show!

For example, I mentioned that *Dead Files* used the YouTube approach to build an audience that eventually sold the show that's now on Travel Channel. Before the Creator went this route, producers rejected the show across the board. They simply couldn't see the concept as a hit show!

But then the Creator started shooting short, 10-minute episodes of the show that aired as a Web Series on YouTube and eventually caught on…the audience was hooked and they came back to the producers with a 250K viewing audience. The producers could no longer ignore this show – it had a built-in audience and was growing! The show was picked up and the rest is history.

Different Routes to Audience Creation

Obviously, the Internet is the fastest way to build a large audience because the Creator literally has access to millions of potential viewers and only needs a base audience of around 200,000 to get Hollywood's attention.

However, there are other ways to build a grass roots audience. Set a counter on the blog to show how many subscribe and have an interest in the show. This can also be done for websites and even Facebook Likes.

When the Creator Beta tests the show for the presentation package, videotape live reactions to the show RIGHT AFTER THE VIEWING. Capture the audience coming out of the theater (or back room in your house) and let the producer hear their live reactions to the show! Of course, the Creator will want to cherry pick the good takes on the show unless a controversial remark could actually help sell it, then use it! A negative remark about how gross your bug-eating contest show was could actually help sell the show. Don't disregard using negative remarks if they help hype the project.

Unique Routes to Audience Creation

I was recently at a home & garden show at the Pomona Fairplex in Los Angeles, California and a lady (Creator) had a booth set up where she was showing people who passed her booth a 1 minute trailer for a home & garden show and asking them to comment (in writing) about what they liked or didn't like about the show based on what they'd seen in the trailer. But more importantly, she had a separate clipboard (via her iPad) where they could sign a petition-style document that they'd love to see this show on the air.

I asked her if she'd mind telling me how many people had signed the petition in favor of the show. This was at 1:30p.m. The event had started at 9a.m. and was scheduled to close at 5p.m. At this point, she'd amassed 2,302 signatures! This doesn't sound like a lot, but the afternoon was even busier than the morning, so it would be a fair estimate that she probably ended the day with 5,000 signatures!

True, she needs 200,000 minimum to even get a producer to take a nod at the project, but if she combined this number with a YouTube audience, blog, website, Facebook Likes, etc., she has a good chance at reaching the golden # to prove her home & garden show could generate a sustainable, interested audience.

While I was writing this book, a friend who's promoting a TV show on Facebook has been receiving 2,000 like a day. They're coming in so fast and consistently – for 9 days in a row now – that he's already caught the attention of a producer. While 200K is the magic number, a rapid and consistent response can do the trick too. What can I say? In Hollywood, numbers equal a built-in audience and rapid number mean the project has heat!

Why 200,000? It's a number set by producers as a base for consideration for shows. It isn't mandatory. I've seen shows sell without any audience creation, but many are initially passed over because they were good shows, but the producer just couldn't see them with an audience. The Creator then had to go out and find the audience, re-pitch the show to the producer and make the sale.

Why hassle with marketing a pitch for a show before establishing an audience? The Creator can go this route, but walking in with a built-in audience can save the Creator time and expedite the show getting picked up for TV!

Note: I'm sure the booth at the home & garden show costs the lady a few bucks. The Creator considering any of these options will have to weigh the financial costs to determine if it's worth the time and effort.

Fundraisers

Booths and promotional tools toward building an audience can cost money. The Creator could go to local restaurants and ask for meal donations to hold a fundraiser to raise the money needed for the Fairplex booth.

Be prepared to offer something in return of value. If the Creator has a home & garden show, the restaurant that hosted the fundraiser might be spotlighted in an upcoming episode or even featured in the entire episode. I can't think of a restaurant owner who'd miss the chance at free TV advertising that could bring customers to the restaurant for years to come!

❦ PITCH FESTIVALS

The most famous one that could land a Creator a sale is the Hollywood Pitch Festival hosted by Fade In On-Line Magazine. See website at https://fadeinonline.com/hollywood-pitch-festival.

This provides the Creator with over 200 producers to pitch over a 1-3 day period. Yes, the Creator will have to pay to attend and will have to print off the pitch presentation and have the trailer/sizzle reel ready to show on a computer or iPad, but it can be well worth it. Or pass out business cards that include the link to the trailer or sizzle reel.

If the Creator decides to go this route, he/she will have to learn how to verbally pitch a producer IN PERSON. This can be intimidating and many would rather avoid this possibility, but DON'T! Hollywood's a collaborative place and even if the Creator sells the show via a YouTube promotion, he/she will still have to intermingle with the Hollywood elite. There will be lots of meetings before the sale is finalized, talks with studio executives, producers, etc. Learning to pitch can help the Creator become comfortable with the collaborative process.

Use an Actor's Technique

Actors may seem smooth, suave and sleek when delivering their lines, but most started out fumbling and insecure. A technique many of them use to overcome this fear is to practice their lines in front of a mirror.

Use their technique to practice talking about the show. Be careful here. Many Creators make the mistake of talking about the presentation. DON'T DO IT! The goal is to get the producer to look at the presentation. That's why you took so long to carefully put it together.

Instead of feeding the producer all the details outlined in the presentation package, the Creator might say something like, "Bigfoot's out there and I have a presentation package that reveals how my show will find him".

If the Creator has a trailer and sizzle reel, start with that and make it the talking point for the pitch. Warning: Pitch Festivals often have a time limit for pitches, usually only a few minutes per pitch. This won't allow time for a 10-minute sizzle reel or even a 3-minute trailer, but if the Creator has a 1-minute trailer (consider editing a longer trailer specifically for presenting at the festival), then start with this....

...allow the trailer to open up the conversation and let the producer ask the questions. AGAIN, the goal is to get the producer to take a copy of the presentation package.

ADDING AUDIENCE TO PITCHES

If the Creator has built an audience of 200K or more, then add a page in the presentation package that shows the numbers. Don't fake this! Producers can easily check YouTube and other sources to confirm the true numbers and they will confirm it!

Or better yet, open the trailer with text that reads: 200,000 viewers strong and growing! This will immediately get the producer's attention.

This is a Business!

They don't call it show business for no reason. Hollywood producers are looking for the next show that will bring in revenue and pitching a producer a show with a sizeable audience causes them to see the dollar signs – CHA-CHING!

DO NOT add the audience numbers if it's below 200K. Don't waste time with a 10K audience by adding it or mentioning it and saying something stupid like 'Our audience is growing every day!' The producer DOES NOT CARE until the show reaches a certain level. MANY, MANY shows reach the 10K mark. There's nothing special about any number under 200K, so keep that figure in mind. Once the Creator's reached the magic number, keep it up and market the #. The only exception, as already noted, is a situation where the audience #'s are rapidly and consistently growing in a very short period – like a week or less – and it's already created Internet hype.

❦ WORD OF MOUTH

This marketing/pitch technique might seem old school, but a Creator might be surprised to learn his butcher has a cousin at Warner Bros who happens to do reality-TV. I've seen this happen when the Creator least expects it!

Tell everyone everywhere you go about the show. Have a business card to pass out with a link to the trailer or Facebook page.

Offer a referral fee if someone puts you in contact with a Hollywood producer and the show sells to that producer. Make it a flat rate, one-time payment with no perks, like producer credits. And don't pay until you've received funding, then pay the referral fee and move forward. Offering long-term perks can become a nightmare later. Quick cash, then say ADIOS.

If someone does put the Creator in contact with a Hollywood producer, BEFORE submitting the presentation package, get a written FINDER'S FEE CONTRACT put together between you and the referring party outlining the terms of the deal. DO NOT proceed without it.

This book will discuss contracts in a later chapter and how to legally protect the project and the Creator from liability.

❦ KEEP A LOG

A requirement for a copyright lawsuit is that the Creator proves the suspected thief had access to the project's details and had stolen them.

Keep a log! Create an Excel spreadsheet or some other type of log where the date, time and party accessing the pitch presentation (the written version, not just the trailer or sizzle reel) are recorded.

Pitching the idea only to someone DOES NOT count because you can't copyright an idea, only the execution of the idea. That's why I advocate a sales pitch that attempts to get the presentation into the hands of the producer! That's a viable creative item where telling them the show's whole concept could end up with a lawsuit where it's your word against the stealing party. You'll lose because you can't copyright the idea, so don't pitch it – pitch the presentation package instead, then document who sees it.

Doing it this way assures the Creator can keep track of who has viewed the copyrighted material. I'd also advise the Creator to slant trailers and even sizzle reels toward getting the producer to view the presentation package – that's the real selling point and the only viable proof the Creator will have of a violation of a copyright infringement.

I wouldn't advocate having a producer sign an NDA (non-disclosure). That's insulting and it isn't necessary if the Creator's keeping a thorough log. However, if the producer wants the Creator to sign one, then do it! Don't stand in the way of your project because you're paranoid someone will steal it. Take the necessary precautions and get the project out there as much as possible. It could take thousands of views before the Creator gets an offer.

A Word About Theft

It may sound confusing when I tell the Creator the only real protection is the written presentation and verbal pitching could mean giving the idea away. Don't take this too literally. If the Creator has a copyrighted concept, then relax.

In fact, it's very unlikely a Hollywood producer would steal a show because they know the costs of a lawsuit, especially if they lost, could be in the millions, which far exceeds what they could just pay to purchase the show in the first place!

Ironically, the most likely thief of a reality-TV show is that guy down the street or your Uncle's friend who thinks he can do it better than you! Remember, anyone can put together a reality-TV show presentation. That doesn't mean the Creator only pitches the show to producers, but just be aware of where the real threat lies.

Bonus Copyright Note

Add a copyright logo to the presentation, trailer, sizzle reel, etc., so it's in plain view of anyone taking a peek at the project.

✛ MAKE A PITCH PACKAGE REGARDLESS OF BUDGET

Over the years, I've had many would-be Creators argue this point. They believe they don't have to go through the process of creating a pitch presentation for their reality-TV show, filming a trailer or building an audience. They'll just sign up for pitch sites on-line and at festivals and verbally pitch a show.

A Very Bad Idea!

First, under KEEP A LOG I mentioned how the Creator can't copyright an idea, but only the execution of the idea. Pitching an idea only without a proper, copyrighted presentation invites theft! Pitching a show with a presentation reveals you're a real professional with protected material. And it shows that you can deliver the entire concept in a formatted show.

Secondly, if the Creator doesn't have a pitch presentation and a producer has to put one together to present to the studio, I guarantee the title of Creator will be stripped away and given to the producer because he/she is the one who's really putting the show together, NOT YOU! It's just an idea you had, nothing more. This will mean less show credits and financial rewards down the road. Plus, I doubt you'd be entitled to royalty payments, which are the golden goose of these shows. You do plan to make money, right? Then get real. Stop being lazy because working on a reality-TV show can be a daunting task and if you can't even put together a presentation, it's unlikely the producer will want you hanging around with more 'ideas' - the show needs a real Creator!

So no excuses! I've also heard, ' I don't have the funds to put together a fancy presentation package. I have to go with the verbal pitch only'. Again, this is a lazy excuse. At the minimum, I'd recommend putting together a 1-3 page pitch package. It's MANDATORY if the Creator plans to be taken seriously.

CHAPTER FIVE

REALITY-TV SHOW CREATOR

❖ UNDERSTAND THE CREATOR'S POSITION

The Creator of a reality-TV show is different than a screenwriter or even a TV writer. The screenwriter sells a screenplay's copyright to a producer and no longer owns the project, even if he or she is involved in the production. The exception is a writer/producer, but most screenplay sales are outright and are no different than selling a vehicle or a house. It's a clear transfer of ownership.

The TV Writer, in comparison, sells the copyright, but he or she stays aboard the show as its Creator, maintaining the title and residual (royalties) income from subsequent episodes. The Creator of a TV show has a lot of clout in Hollywood and usually has a lot of say in the creative process and how the show will maintain its tone, mood and atmosphere.

The reality-TV Creator has a choice where rights are concerned. The Creator can do an outright sale, like the screenwriter or stay aboard and help run the show like the TV writer.

Pros & Cons of An Outright Sale

If the Creator doesn't work in the industry, it might seem tempting to walk into town, make a reality-TV sale and take the check to the bank. While reality-TV can be lucrative, it doesn't pay that much upfront. The show would need to become a hit or find a solid audience before the Creator will see a golden goose sitting on the front lawn, but a patient Creator can stick with it and reap the rewards.

After all, would you rather be working for someone else, making him or her wealthy, when you can work your own show and make yourself rich?

However, if the Creator doesn't have an overwhelming enthusiasm for the project, and/or doesn't want to be the boss, then an outright sale might be for the best. BUT remember, you're giving up a lot. An outright sale will mean you'll be lucky to receive any residuals (royalties) on the show's future episodes and if you do they will be minimal to say the least.

Unlike screenplay sales where the producer will have minimal or no future contact with the original writer, the reality-TV Creator is expected to stay aboard for the long haul. If you opt out, it'll make a second sale very difficult.

Pros & Cons of Staying Aboard

If the Creator sticks with the show after the sale, then you'll basically become like a show runner, and you'll be the boss. You'll make all the decisions on filming, edits, locations, permits, catering, travel, casting, etc. It might sound like a lot, but you'll have a studio-level show runner heading up the entire show. This person will make sure you learn to do things right and help you along the way.

Word of Warning: If you're not an organized person and you find the job of putting together a presentation package daunting, then you'll probably crash and burn. Running a reality-TV show is a logistical job requiring handling of multiple things at once in an organized and precise manner. Forget one thing or slopping it over and you can bring your own production to a halt.

Case in point: I know a Creator who'd never worked in the biz before and thought he could run his show better than anyone. He refused to listen to the advice and teachings of the show runner appointed by the studio. He got caught up in getting his crew to the location on time, but forgot to get the proper permits. He'd put in for them with City Hall, but they weren't finalized. The crew showed up on time, but local authorities shut down the production and fined the producers for filming without proper permits. It was a costly lesson!

Another consideration is the time and potential travel involved in a reality-TV show. Like other TV shows, reality-TV films for several straight months a year (or often referred to as a season), then everyone goes on hiatus with months off at a time. Doesn't this sound fantastic? Having months off! But during the filming, there's little time for anything else. The days can be long, sometimes 10-12 hours and show runners & Creators often work through the weekends to keep up with the busy pace.

The Creator will also need to film on location, wherever that may be. If it's a monster show, like *Finding Bigfoot*, the Creator could end up traveling from one end of the country to the other during a season. If you've always wanted to travel, this might sound like the dream job, but if you have a wife and two kids at home, it could turn into a nightmare.

But considering most reality-TV shows have a fairly short shelf life, say 1-3 years, you're more likely to cash in, work temporarily, and then return home. If the Creator is smart, he/she won't wait around to see if the show becomes a hit, but will start looking for other shows to pitch to Hollywood. You'll be in a spot to get priority pitches!

Multiple Shows in the Works

Yes, the Creator will be busy working on the original show that sold, but a smart Creator will pitch a second, third, fourth, fifth, etc., show to Hollywood in the hopes of landing another reality-TV spot if and when the first show fizzles out – and most do!

Josh Gates from *Destination Truth* has gone on to create several other reality-TV shows: including *Expedition Unknown* and *Legend Has It*. While other shows have created spin-offs related to the original series, like *The Real Housewives of Beverly Hills* that's spun off into *The Real Housewives of Atlanta*, etc.

Don't bother trying to pitch multiple shows up front even if you have a spin-off or another reality-TV show in mind. The studio won't bite. The Creator will have to prove the original show has

teeth before the producer and/or studio will put money into a second series, but if the original show draws an audience, start pitching! Don't wait just because you're busy producing the first show. At least get the second show's presentation package ready. Going from one show to the next or having multiple reality-TV shows running at once is the way to early retirement! Don't worry, if you have several running at once, the studio will let you pick which one you want to focus on as the primary show and assign show runners to the other ones. Now that's what I call a dream job!

It's also the way to stay relevant in the industry, make money and here's the best part of all....

Residual Payments

Besides the upfront money the Creator receives for the reality-TV show and the monies for subsequent episodes, when the Creator retire from the industry he/she can still receive money from the show! How? It's called residual payments. In can get complicated, but here's the basics of how it works: every time the show airs anywhere in the world, the Creator's entitled to a payment! It might be a small check or a big one, depending on the country the show aired in, air time and residual entitlements based on the Creator's studio contract.

If the show airs in primetime, which is 8p.m. to 11p.m., Monday through Friday, that's the bigger bucks, with other dates/times receiving smaller increments in the residual category. The unions (WGA, SAG & DGA) keep track of this and make sure you get what's coming to you on a quarterly basis. I personally know producers and actors who live off their residuals. Wasn't it totally worth those 10-12 hour days you did for 3 years in a row? Off course, the Creator only receives on-going residuals if and when the show airs. Some shows die out, while others air in countries around the world for years to come.

Credits

The TV credit you'll receive for being the original creator of a reality-TV show is CREATOR, but can also include producer (often referred to as show runner). Creators often go on to put some of their own money back into their projects. In this case, you'd receive an Executive Producer credit, which means you're the moneyman (or woman) behind the show.

❖ CREATOR'S MANDATORY MUST DO'S

It's imperative the Creator understand what he/she must do during the setup process outlined in this book. Yes, the Creator needs a reality-TV pitch presentation and it'll be great if the Creator can also come up with a visual example of the show, like a trailer and/or sizzle reel, but there's more to it than that.

In earlier chapters, we reviewed a key factor in selling the reality-TV show = Characters (otherwise referred to as the cast) and how unique personalities can make or break a show. But this can quickly fall apart and become a legal nightmare if the Creator didn't handle the legal logistics of signing up characters/cast for the show.

Case in Point: A young, African American man knew all the street talent in a 5-block radius in NYC, from musicians to actors, etc. He put together a reality-TV show based on their lives panhandling and struggling for the big break. It was pretty darn good and a big studio quickly picked up his reality-TV show, but when they asked him to drop off the release forms to their legal department he didn't know what they were talking about.

Release Forms

The rule is simple, anyone the Creator interviews behind or in front of the camera and the Creator plans to use any part of that interview in the pitch presentation and/or reality-TV show, the Creator MUST get a release form from that party. This form allows the Creator (and the studio) to use the interviewees voice, image, information, etc., in any media format.

Unfortunately, when the young African American man went back to NYC to obtain the release forms, word had gotten around the streets about his big studio deal and all the players involved wanted unrealistic salaries, plus perks or they wouldn't come aboard. The project flopped before it ever got off the ground.

The release form IS NOT A CONTRACT for the person to come aboard. It just allows the Creator to use the information, visual or otherwise, obtained from the interviewee. The Creator can wait until after the sale of the show and let the show runner negotiate union rates with the players, but get that one-page release form signed before even speaking to the person on/off camera.

Go to www.FilmSourcing.com to download a FREE Release Form. For cast or anyone appearing in front of the camera, download the *Talent Release Form.*

If the Creator plans to use a specific location in the trailer and/or sizzle reel or even in the presentation, it's a good idea to obtain a *Location Release Form*, which covers the Creator's liability should the location's owner claims any time of damage due to cast, filming, etc.

Extra Note: This site also has budget sheets and other handy tools the Creator might find helpful in the process of putting together the Reality-TV show presentation.

Pay for Cast

What the cast will receive depends on many factors in reality-TV and the Creator would be a fool to make promises up front. Just get the release form, then when the project sells, let the show runner negotiate the rates of pay based on the studio's decision when and where to air the show, etc. If a cast member wants guaranteed money and/or perks written up in a contract before they'll let the Creator use them in the show, MOVE ON! This person will be a pain to work with later and could wreak havoc on the production if and when they don't get everything they want all the time. I've seen it happen repeatedly. The Creator can avoid these future problems by identifying these individuals up front and taking them off the potential casting list.

If this person is the Creator's potential star, then get everything in writing in conjunction with the show runner, sit down and read it aloud and make sure the star is in agreement BEFORE starting to film. If the star raises a fuss later, just refer him or her back to the contract. Do not argue points or you'll lose. Just tell them to refer to their contract and walk away! Don't let them hold you or your show hostage! This is another good reason to have a second show in the works and the reason it's mandatory to get everything in writing.

Understand Perks

A perk is an extra bonus that's above and beyond the normal pay. It can be anything from leaving early on Fridays to a chef for a pet lizard (wish I were kidding, but I've seen this!). Reality-TV shows function on limited budgets, so perks may be few, if any. But I'd encourage the Creator to try to get a few for the cast to keep them locked into the show. The Creator will have to get the perks approved by the show runner. It can be anything from 2-hour lunches on Wednesdays to leaving early on Friday, extra packs of bottled soda for their star trailer or being allowed to bring a family pet on set. Try to make it something everyone gets so there's no fussing and feuding later.

What about the Creator's perks? Creators often get built-in perks, like a studio parking spot (that's a coveted thing), a personal chef, an assistant for the show's administrative needs and to pick up the dry cleaning, a deluxe star trailer with bed, TV, private bathroom, sitting area, etc., and probably other personal considerations, like a hairstylists, etc. This is assuming the show can afford such things. Most have these levels of perks for the Creator or at least a few perks, but I have seen shows with none of these where the Creator camps out in RV's with the cast and crew or they stay at a local Best Western and only get breakfast if they partake in the complimentary continental breakfast served daily until 9a.m.

The Creator and the Cast perks depend on one thing and that's the show's budget, which at first could be minimal and later blossom into star trailers and an on-set chef. It also depends on how well the show is doing once it hits the air. Is it generating buzz, bringing in an audience or getting news feed? A show that shoots up in popularity will quickly find its limited budget expanded by the studio.

Photographs & Random Footage

One of the areas a Creator might accidentally overlook in terms of release forms is the photography. A smart Creator will be taking tons of pictures everywhere he/she goes while putting together the reality-TV show's pitch presentation. Since the presentation isn't itself being sold, the Creator can widely use images of people, places, etc., without having to obtain release forms from the parties being shown. The exception is a celebrity who's image might hold copyright infringements if used in the document.

However, if the Creator plans to use any of the photographs later in the show and a person or persons appears in the photograph, the Creator will need a release form from that party in order to use the photograph in the show. This also applies to random footage taken during the setup process. If the Creator plans to use it later and hasn't obtained a release form from everyone who appears in the footage, it can NOT be used.

Don't drive yourself crazy trying to get release forms from everyone in every photograph or piece of footage. Imagine if you're taking pictures at an amusement park. It would be unrealistic to assume you'd be able to get a release form from 200 hundred people who appear in the photograph or footage.

Show runners often put up signs that read something like:

This area is being used to photograph and record video, film and digital footage in connection with the production (List show title here). By your presence in this area, you acknowledge that you have been informed that you may be photographed and recorded as part of the release in home video and/or any and all media now known or hereafter devised in perpetuity, throughout the universe and the advertising and publicity thereof. Further, by your presence here, you grant your permission for your likeness and voice to be included therein without compensation. If you do not wish to be photographed, recorded or appear under these conditions, you should leave the area immediately. Thank you for your cooperation.

Be selective and know your show well enough to know what you will and won't use in the future. Cherry pick and only get the release forms from the most important photographs and/or footage and keep it as part of a collection to use for the show. Just so you know, there's no compensation paid to the person(s) in the photograph or footage. If someone wants money before they'll sign a release form, then don't use that footage or photograph. If you start paying for every image on photographs or footage, the show will go broke. Of course, we're only referring to images the Creator has taken. The Creator will need to pay for stock footage.

However, if you get someone who's insistent, I've seen Creators offer a copy of the episode on DVD. That's the way to go, but do not pay! If this happens, get their contact information and give it to the assistant and if the photograph or footage they appear in airs, then send them the DVD copy, as promised. If you pay and others find out, you could be opening the show to legal liability.

Interviews – The Casting Test

Interviews were mentioned in an earlier chapter, but this requires a revisit here. First, the Creator knows he/she MUST obtain a release form for the interviewee so the information collected, whether verbal or via videotape can be used later. That's mandatory!

Always try to go for the videotaped interview. If the person hesitates or balks at the idea of being interviewed, mention that this would be a regular part of the show. If they still hesitate, then go to an off-camera interview, but keep this in mind that this isn't a person the Creator can use later in front of the camera for the show.

Why not? Think about it. If the person is hesitant now when it's only you and them in the room, there's no way you're getting that person in front of a camera with an entire crew aiming cameras at him or her with sound booms dangling overhead and lights piercing their eyeballs. It just isn't going to happen!

Don't fret because this is important to know upfront. If the Creator thought someone would make a great star, but that person is camera shy, it's best to learn this up front rather than after you've sold the show to Hollywood and you discover the show's a no-go because the star won't appear before a camera.

Dealing with Camera Shy Cast

If it's evident from your arrival that the person will run from being in front of the camera, then ease in to it. Do a sit down interview with no cameras, just take notes and ask if you can get a photograph or two. And the release form! Tell them you'd like to do more research on the project and see if you can follow them around for a day, an hour or whatever suits their schedule.

When the Creator shows up for the 'research', bring the camera, but tell them you're using it to follow yourself or to shoot the location, etc., keeping them out of the equation. Creators will often discover that by the end of the day, the person is literally placing himself or herself in front of the camera. In today's world where self-taken photos rule, people usually end up being less camera shy than they original thought they were and the Creator ends up with a star who loves the camera. And it was all because you knew better than to pressure the person and they won't be wise to the fact that you eased them in front of the camera in a clever way.

If this doesn't work, then scratch this cast member off your list because if you can't get them in front of a camera, then you have nothing to work with.

❖ UNDERSTAND TRAILERS & SIZZLE REELS

The book has referenced these two terms already and spoken of them in general terms, but in this chapter we're going to review the in-depth meaning of both and how any Creator, regardless of budget can create a visual landscape to help up the chances at a sale of their reality-TV show.

This topic has been put under the Creator's chapter because it's a vital tool in the Creator's marketing arsenal.

First, what are trailers and sizzle reels? Most of you are familiar with the term 'trailer' because they're used to advertise a new feature film currently playing at a local theater. They're usually 1-3 minutes long and give just enough highlights or teasers to entice a moviegoer to drive to the theater, pay money, buy popcorn and watch the feature film on a giant, silver screen!

A sizzle reel, on the other hand, isn't something used to advertise to the public. It's a reel put together by a show's Creator to highlight and tease a producer into purchasing the show to air on the networks. Think of it as a longer-formatted trailer and unlike the movie trailer, the sizzle reel usually runs from 5-10 minutes in length and is much more in-depth in terms of information. The information goes beyond the highlights and teasers, usually including things like cast interviews, location previews, etc.

However, regardless of the time difference between a trailer and a sizzle reel, the objective is the same = to sell the show. Don't get bogged down with information overload. The goal is to sell the show, not tell the show! Think of these two selling tools like the many advertisements seen on TV daily. They provide just enough information and hype to make the consumer want to purchase the product. The show is the product! And the producer is the consumer you want to entice to buy it!

Cost Considerations

Here comes the part where the Creator claims he/she can't afford to put together a trailer or sizzle reel because they don't have access to the millions of dollars they'd need to pay for it.

Say what? Yes, we're all used to seeing those fancy movie trailers, but the people putting them together, usually studios, are paying top dollar union rates and star salaries, etc. Wipe all of that out and learn a few new tricks and you can put together a trailer for under $1,000 dollars. In fact, I've put together trailers for as low as $300 that were beautifully edited and very professional looking and you can do the same!

The Low-Cost, High Quality Trailer

Let's explore how to put together a low-cost, yet high quality trailer that will take Hollywood by storm. First, we live in a modern world where HD cameras are everywhere. You probably have one built-in your smart phone. That's where you start. High Definition (HD) is the key!

Use it to shoot every thing from the inception of the project forward. I realize you're unlikely to be a film school graduate, but that's okay. I'm going to teach you a few simple tricks to use for filming:

- ○ Don't center the person or object in the frame. We're used to doing this for birthday parties, etc. That's for family and cloud photo albums, not for film. Off-center the subject in the frame slightly to the left. This gives depth perception and will make the footage look like it was shot by a Hollywood director.

○ Pay close attention to background noise and echoes. We take these for granted in our daily lives, but passing vehicles, overhead planes and rooms with an echo can distort a wonderful piece of footage and leave the Creator without a quality sound track. The Creator can literally get away with using the audio from the HD camera if he/she pays close attention and takes steps to avoid the background noise.

○ Lighting is another area that can make or break the footage. Use the camera's built-in light to light the subject or person, if possible. Watch the angle of the sun for exterior shots being sure to keep it behind you and watch for unforeseen shadows that can creep into the footage, including your shadow. Take a close look at how the image or subject looks. Does it look like something you'd see on your TV at home? If not, why? Is it too dark, and then try to lighten the surroundings. If it's too light, then move to another location because excess lighting can be difficult to block out.

○ Use the HD camera's built-in editing functions to lighten, darken, and to enhance contrast and sharpness to the footage before downloading it to a computer.

If the Creator follows these simple directing rules, he/she should be able to get some great footage that looks high quality and can be used for the trailer and/or sizzle reel and virtual zero cost.

Note: iPad cameras are also routinely used to take HD photographs and even for filming video! It's a great alternative to a phone and because the screen's wider/bigger, the Creator will get a better view of the finished look.

But don't get carried away. You're not a film director. Only use your own HD camera (or iPad) for things like interviews and a few shots of locations, etc. For the majority of the trailer and/or sizzle reels,

I want you to rely on professional footage known as stock footage that is used by many reality-TV shows.

Understand Stock Footage

Stock footage is used by many reality-TV shows, like investigative series, etc. Check the credits and you'll see a listing for stock footage from places like Getty Images, Shutter Fly, Pond 5, DreamsTime, etc.

Stock footage is random pieces of film footage, sound, music, etc., shots by amateurs and pros alike and sold and/or licensed via an internet site that specializes in such materials.

These are stock footage sites available on the Internet where the show's Creator can purchase HD footage (recommend HD1080) at a reasonable price that can be added to footage the Creator took with their own HD camera to create a high-quality looking trailer. The footage taken with your camera is zero cost and the stock footage can run a couple hundred up to thousands, but don't get too elaborate. Images from stock footage are often spliced or repeated in trailers and/or sizzle reels to create pacing and save funds by stretching out their usage.

If the Creator already has an idea, whether you've begun the process of putting together the reality-TV show pitch presentation or not, start going through the stock footage on websites and finding pieces that you can use in a trailer or sizzle reel. Open an account and put the footage into the cart – you can delete it later, but start stockpiling footage you might be able to use for your concept. Some Creators discover most of the footage they'll need is right there in front of them and mixed with a few well-shot interviews, the Creator has a professional looking 1-3 minute trailer that will cost on average between $300 to $1,000 dollars! Who says you have to pay millions? Only studios put out that kind of money for a trailer. Indie filmmakers know how to do it for pennies on the dollar!

Edit the Trailer

Every Creator would love to hire a professional film editor, but that will break the bank and the $1,000, low-cost budget. Here are a few options:

- ○ Learn to do it yourself and purchase a simple movie making software package for PC or Mac. It can be a fun adventure.

  But if you're all thumbs when it comes to computers, then keep reading.

- ○ Ask a high school or college student to help you put it together in exchange for a few pizzas, movie tickets or a few bucks. Or give them a credit on the trailer and they can use it as a sample to show others their film work. Lots of film students will do this at zero or little cost to you. Put a free ad on Craiglist under GIGS in the FILM CREW section. The ad should read something like "Seeking Film Student for 1-3 minute Trailer in Exchange for a credit, movie tickets and a pizza!" Other places to put up ads: college campuses, post offices, libraries, and grocery stores.

Don't turn this into a big Hollywood production. Keep things simple with a few filmed interviews, 3-10 pieces of stock footage and the goal of a 1-3 minute trailer and try for the 1-minute trailer first. Less is more in Hollywood and a Creator can condense a concept down and intrigue a producer into purchasing it from a 1-minute trailer, then Hollywood will remember you and want to work with you in the future. Besides, the Creator can take the 1-minute trailer to a pitch without fear of running out of time because the trailer is short enough to allow time for the verbal portion of the pitch, even in a festival setting where pitch time is limited.

Watch every trailer you can. Links to trailers for film and TV can be found on www.imdb.com. Make note of how the trailer entices you to purchase the movie ticket or watch the TV show. The Creator needs to do this with his project. Do not tell us the story; sell it to us! Put on a salesman's hat and focus on teasing or hyping the project just enough to make the sale! The details can come later.

If you're still not sure how to put all this together, write it up in script format and use the script to create the trailer. Since the rule is one page equals one minute of film time, the script shouldn't be more than a few pages long. It's often easier to see how something will look in the final phase when it's on paper first.

Voice Over Actors

A nice touch to a trailer is hearing that deep, male voice narrating over the moving images. We're used to hearing it in film trailers and if the Creator uses this technique is his/her trailer, it'll automatically elevate the trailer to a professional level. It's not mandatory, but it'll really make a huge difference.

Yes, voice over actors can be expensive, but I've negotiated non-union rates for as low as $300 for a 1-minute trailer = one page script. It was worth the money. Find an actor that can record his own voice and send you the audio recording. This will save the expense of renting studio space to create the recording. Where do you find these actors? Put a free ad on Backstage.com and you'll get more resumes that you can handle. Listen to the voices and pick one that mimics the deep, male tones we're used to hearing. It's a nifty trick that can fool a producer into thinking you've spent tens of thousands of dollars on the trailer when you never went over the $1K budget. The ad should read: "Seeking Non-Union Voice Over Actor for 1-3 minute trailer $300 Flat Rate Compensation. Must be able to supply recording."

Extra Note: If a producer or anyone ever asks what you spent on the trailer – DO NOT TELL THEM! That's your creative secret weapon. Keep it to yourself!

Add Up the Costs

The total tally for the low-cost trailer will look something like the following:

$600 Stock Footage

$300 Voice Over Actor

$100 Editor (pizzas, etc.)

$1,000 TOTAL COST

The Creator may or may not use $600 in stock footage. I've often come in under $200. If you're going above $600, you might be making too many selections for a 1-3 minute trailer. Simplify and economize and you can make a super low-budget, high quality trailer.

Stock Footage Usage Rights

When the Creator purchases stock footage from a site like Getty Images or Pond5.com, the Creator is purchasing a license to use the footage for promotional purposes only, which is royalty free. If the footage is ever used in the show, the Creator will have to pay a royalty payment based on the site's rules and regulations. Please read each sites rules/regulations carefully to make sure you understand potential future costs.

For the purpose of the promotional trailer or sizzle reel, the Creator only has to worry about the licensing fee, which is paid up front before the Creator can download the footage. Be sure to keep a copy of this purchase, the Creator may need to prove to sites like YouTube that the copyrighted footage has been licensed for promotional use.

Music Usage

Stock footage sites offer royalty free pieces of music the Creator can license along with footage. Only select ONE piece of music that best suits the tone, mood and atmosphere of the show. Do NOT select apiece based on your personal taste in music. The Creator's love for heavy Metallic music could ruin a trailer for a food show about taco trucks, unless the taco truck operators are tattooed, tough guys, then maybe it would work. Stick with simple, instrumental pieces that could help attract an audience.

Audio pieces are usually extremely cheap, so purchasing one piece of music for the trailer and/or sizzle reel will be cost effective, and there's no reason why the Creator can't use the same piece of music for both the trailer and the sizzle reel.

The Sizzle Reel

Putting together the sizzle reel is the same as putting together the trailer; the difference is the length and the costs. A sizzle reel is a longer sales pitch/trailer for the project that should run between 5-10 minutes. This doesn't sound like a long time, but even a minute in film is a long time....you'll see what I mean when you start to edit your first trailer.

Many Creators have asked me why they'd need a sizzle reel if they have a trailer. You don't. I'd recommend doing one or the other. Sizzle reels have become popular lately with producers. They like to see a sizzle reel because it shows them that the Creator can present the project in a longer format and keep it entertaining. Where a trailer might be all fluff with little substance.

The costs will be more than the trailer, probably ranging closer to $3k because it's literally 3 times the length of the trailer.

If the Creator can only choose between one of the two, I'd recommend going with the trailer. If costs are a major consideration, then go with the 1-minute, $1K trailer. Put it on a credit card or do a fundraiser on-line. It's that important. If you can't do this, it's okay. This book gives the Creator a variety of options starting at zero costs.

A Word of Caution: I've seen many Creators ruin the sizzle reel by loading up the longer run time with cast interviews. This can get really boring to watch! Get creative with the editing. Show faster paced pieces of footage overlapping while the interviewee speaks and keep a visually entertaining pacing going throughout the sizzle reel.

❦ UNDERSTAND BUDGETS & LOCATIONS

This chapter has been primarily dedicated to things the Creator will need to know before making a sale, but this portion will be dedicated to an area that the Creator technically doesn't need to know until after the show's been purchased. However, it's imperative to understand if the Creator wants to become a success and keep the show running without budget breakdowns that can quickly sink the ship.

Reality-TV Show Budgets

As mentioned earlier in the book, reality-TV budgets per episode tend to be low. Even episodic TV shows run with budgets averaging between $1 to $4million dollars. Some TV shows do have super high budgets, like $10million, but they are few and far between the norm.

Reality-TV shows can range from the money it takes to fly a Ghost Hunting crew to a location up to much larger budgets for cast, crew, locations, hotels, food, salaries, etc. Most episodes are shot for a few hundred thousand or less. Profits come later from advertising dollars and residual payments.

How much will vary by show. The reason I'm mentioning this is because when the Creator is first putting together a reality-TV show pitch presentation, they can inadvertently put themselves out of the game by making the show seem too high budget. For example, I had a friend that put together a pretty nifty ghost hunting show all shot at one location, but the technology he was planning to use was like NASA and would have costs a fortune to run, maintain and insure. He priced the show out of the market.

Here are some things to avoid that could price the reality-TV show out of the marketplace:

- Show requiring or involving explosions.
- Show shot entirely where the weather's horrible (*Ice Road Truckers* is an exception, but keep this in mind).
- Show with a huge cast. Keep it down to 10 or under.
- Show with too many locations per episode. Stick to 1-3 locations per episodes, preferably one.
- Show requiring expensive re-enactments of crimes, etc. Keep the concept low budget in nature.
- Show involving locations that are extremely expensive to film in, like airports where the costs can run up to $10K a day! Check with local film offices with city/state for pricing.
- Show involving big action scenes, like car races, motorcycle races, cross country marathons. These can involve danger stakes and be extremely expensive to insure making these types of show unattractive to producers.

All of these considerations have shows that have broken the rules and gone on to be huge successes, but they are very difficult to sell on the spec market. That's the market where the Creator has put together a show without first consulting with Hollywood and getting the go ahead and has instead opted to speculate on the show's potential for a sale.

Understand Locations

Locations and budgets go hand-in-hand in a reality-TV show. If a show doesn't rely on the location as a selling point, like a show involving finding the Loch Ness monster, which would be filmed primarily at one lake, then don't move the show around.

Keep it confined to a one kitchen like in *Hells Kitchen* with a few sidebar minutes of rewards where the cast are seen going for a day of adventures based on a recent win. But the majority of the show is filmed on one stage or at one location, which significantly reduces location costs. Anytime the Creator has to move a crew or cast, there are going to be significant costs involved. Always keep that in mind.

If the show relies on traveling to different locations, like a show where a team's hunting for a swamp monster that's been spotted around the globe, then keep each episode to one location. In episode one, the team might travel to the backwoods of Alabama, and then in episode two the team ventures to the Florida everglades. One location per episode is the way to keep costs down and still travel the map.

A word of advice: Try to keep the travels inside the USA at least until the show gets an audience, then the team can venture out into other countries because more funding will be available for exotic locales and the show will be able to afford the cost of insurance for international travel.

Final Word

All this information may seem overwhelming, but keep things simple. Less is more in Hollywood no matter how elaborate the finished product looks!

Think in terms of getting things done with the least so later the show will be rewarded the most! The competition will be fierce. My best advice: Stay true to your voice, keep things simple and have fun.

CHAPTER SIX

CREATE LOW ($0 FUNDS), MEDIUM & HIGH-BUDGET PRESENTATIONS

This book has helped the aspiring Creator of a reality-TV show understand how to put together different concepts into a packaged format to present to the entertainment industry. Reality-TV packages can be very simplistic or elaborate. How much goes into the package should depend on the Creator's budget.

If the Creator has enough to put together a more elaborate package, I'd recommend doing so. If the Creator can't afford it, then stick with what works and won't break the Creator's bank account.

Regardless of budget, a Creator should be able to put together a professional package to market. This chapter is going to go through putting together a package with a low budget, a medium budget and a high budget.

Please READ ALL BUDGETS, regardless of which budget your project falls under. Creators often get ideas from the other presentation budgets and even if it's outside their budget, they can come up with creative ways to make it happen within their limitations. And it's always good to know what types of things can go into higher budgeted packages.

✥ THE LOW-BUDGET PRESENTATION PACKAGE

If the Creator is living paycheck to paycheck, being asked to put together even a $1K trailer could discourage the Creator from even trying to sell a concept to Hollywood. STOP! You don't have to put a dime into the presentation package if you can't afford it!

Why? When reality-TV became trendy in Hollywood and everyone was jumping on board, there wasn't a clear way to present the material. At first, it was done via a verbal pitch, but producers soon discovered that even the most exciting sounding pitches didn't make the cut when put to the test of becoming a packaged show.

So producers started asking for a one-sheet. This was already being used for screenplay presentations and seemed like the best way to present the reality-TV show. Basically, it's one-sheet of paper that works as a sales pitch of the show with a title, logline, brief synopsis, teaser, and whatever information the Creator deemed relevant to selling the show. The only difference is that unlike screenplay one-sheets, the reality-TV one-sheet allowed room for photography and Creators often added a picture that highlighted the show. The picture could be a boxed-in frame style or even encompass the entire background of the page; either way was acceptable.

While this type of presentation isn't as widely used today, it is still widely accepted, but in a longer format (can be up to 20-pages) and encompasses the material the Creator learned to put together earlier in this book. Most $0 to low-budget presentation are 1-3 pages, but they can be expanded up to 20-pages, but it's recommended to keep a limit at 20-pages. This isn't a book presentation; it's a presentation for a reality-TV show.

This will still require the Creator to do the basic legwork, like putting together the concept details, interviewing prospects for the show, setting up the rules & regulations for game shows and providing all the relevant information to entice a producer to purchase the show.

Here's a list of what the Creator of the low-budget ($0 money) presentation package will need:

- ➤ Determine the Show's Series Type (See Chapter Two)
- ➤ Put the presentation package together (See Chapter Three: Crafting the Reality-TV Show).

- ➤ Prepare the Presentation (See Chapter Four: Prepare a Reality-TV Presentation)
- ➤ Have a standard query letter ready to go (See Chapter Four: Prepare a Reality-TV Presentation)

Dealing with Cost Items

If anything in the Chapters outlined above cost money, skip it and put together as much of the presentation as possible. Don't pay for stock photography, but it is recommended that the Creator attempt to add photographs to the presentation. Take your own with a smartphone or a borrowed HD camera.

If the Creator doesn't have a computer program, like Power Point or Photoshop, to put the presentation package together, ask friends, co-workers, high school kids or college interns if they can assist you. The Creator might have to put out for a pizza, but it'll keep the costs extremely low. Make it homemade pizza and really economize.

Running off hard copies of the presentation can be expensive. Recommend the Creator send the presentation as an Adobe Acrobat .pdf format to producers via email. Most software programs, like Power Point and Photoshop, will allow the Creator to make a .pdf file. This function is usually found under the FILE tab. Look for Save as pdf. If you don't see this, then click on the PRINT tab and select PRINT AS PDF. This function will allow the Creator to make a .pdf file of the presentation that can be attached to emails at no cost to the Creator.

Copyright & WGA expenses can be over $100. If you can't afford both, then at least register the presentation with the Writer's Guild of America (WGA) for $20. DO NOT MARKET until this is done! When you accumulate funds at a later date, be sure to apply for the U.S. Copyright.

Marketing sites recommended in this book can get pricey. For this budget, it's recommended the Creator stick with $0 marketing options, like Facebook, creating a blog and word of mouth. Or start a Go Fund Me page and raise money to attend a pitch festival with the festival, plane ride, hotel and food expenses covered.

Release forms can also cost money to print and the Creator will have to have signed hard copies. Only run off a few for now. Recommend 5-10. Run them off at home, if you have a printer or ask a friend, co-worker or someone else if they can run a few off for you.

Final Word

This package only requires the Creator put the reality-TV pitch presentation together for marketing. When a producer asks for the presentation, send this package. If they ask if you have a link for a trailer or sizzle reel, be honest and just say not at this time. If the producer hesitates at all, use a sales technique on him (or her) and say something like, "I'm starting to send out the package and I'd love for you to be one of the first to see it." No producer can pass on being the first to see a reality-TV show presentation. They know if they turn down the chance to look at it and another producer picks up the show, they'll be significantly hurting their own career.

❖ THE MEDIUM BUDGET PRESENTATION PACKAGE

If the Creator can afford a little money toward the package, then go with the medium budget presentation package. This consists of putting together a presentation package of 1-20 pages and a $1K trailer (running approximately 1-3 minutes). Adding the trailer to the package gives the Creator two advantages: 1) The Creator has a visual representation to show the producer, which is powerful in a Show Don't Tell town like Hollywood 2) The Creator can use the trailer to build a verifiable audience to gain the attention of a producer who might otherwise pass on the concept.

Start by putting together the Presentation Package as outlined in the following chapters:

➤ Determine the Show's Series Type (See Chapter Two)
➤ Put the presentation package together (See Chapter Three: Crafting the Reality-TV Show).
➤ Prepare the Presentation (See Chapter Four: Prepare a Reality-TV Presentation)
➤ Have a standard query letter ready to go (See Chapter Four: Prepare a Reality-TV Presentation)

There will be a few cost items, which I suggest the Creator add to the package's overall costs. The added costs consist of stock footage, stock photography, and hard copies of the presentation, release forms, plus copyright & WGA registrations. The Creator can also decide whether or not to try to market to on-line websites and absorb the cost. Sit down and add up the costs ahead of time to make sure the project doesn't go over budget or run out of funding.

The trailer shouldn't cost more than $1K. If it does, the Creator has overspent in areas like stock footage and needs to cut back and economize. The rest of the package shouldn't exceed another $1K, inclusive of copyright & WGA registrations, website marketing, hard copies, etc. If the writer's overall cost is exceeding $2K, then something is wrong. Go back and check the budget for areas that are eating up the costs and make cuts!

CREATE THE $1K TRAILER

AFTER the Creator has put the presentation package together, then start the trailer. It's extremely important to have the entire presentation package completed BEFORE starting the trailer.

It can be exciting to have an idea and want to get right to the heart of the concept by jumping straight into the trailer, but this is an amateurish mistake. Why? Because taking the time to create the presentation package weeds out things that work and don't work in the logistical framework of the show. If the Creator does the trailer first, then does the presentation package, the Creator might discover the trailer highlights areas that no longer work or would hinder the show's chances at a sale. And this could cost the Creator significantly, especially if the Creator has to redo the entire trailer!

Act like a professional and go through the tedious legwork of putting the presentation package together. This assures the Creator has a solid foundation from which to explore visual presentation options, prepare queries/sales letters, verbal pitches, etc.

To learn how to put the trailer together for $1K or under, go to Chapter 5: The Reality-TV Show Creator, see section Understanding Trailers and Sizzle Reels.

BUILDING A YOUTUBE AUDIENCE

The last part of the medium budget presentation package is building a YouTube Audience. Once the Creator has the trailer edited and has Beta tested it with an audience, it's time to go wide!

Open a YouTube Account at www.YouTube.com and follow the setup instructions to submit the video to YouTube. Make sure the viewing options allow the Public to view the trailer without requiring passwords or other protections. The Creator wants the trailer to go viral!

Open the account and upload the video. If YouTube makes any fuss about copyrighted material on the trailer, indicate to them that you've purchased the licensing rights to use the material and give them the name of the stock footage company you used for the footage or music. The Creator may be required to submit proof of the licensing rights. Be sure to keep copies of the purchases from stock footage companies in a file, ready to go.

Make sure to have a counter running that not only shows how many Likes and Dislikes the trailer received, but how many people actually viewed the trailer. This part is vital because the Creator will need to show a producer verifiable proof that the show has a following or at least a strong interest from the general public.

Make sure the trailer is 100% ready before uploading to YouTube. I knew a Creator who kept editing his trailer and uploading a new version every couple days, thereby wiping out the counter, which already had over 500 views. When he was ready to market, the reset counter was 500 views away from the golden 200,000 views to attract a producer. He had messed up his own audience by jumping the gun and uploading a trailer that wasn't ready for viewing.

Final Word

This is probably the package I'd recommend most Creators go for because it consists of the two, main parts required to really nail down a sale; the written and visual pitch! It gives the Creator a lot to work with and assures the Creator has learned how to properly putting together a presentation for a reality-TV show.

✣ THE HIGH BUDGET PRESENTATION PACKAGE

If the Creator has a substantial budget of $2K or above and is willing to risk putting it into the reality-TV package that may or may not sell, then go for it! This package is one usually seen by existing Creators of other shows who have the funds from their existing shows to put together elaborate packages to present to producers and studio executives in the hopes of landing a second, third or even fourth show on the air.

This presentation package consists of the following:

- A Written Presentation Package (1-20 pages).
- A trailer (1-3 minutes) with $2-3K budget range or higher.
- A movie-style poster.

- A sizzle reel (expanded trailer up to 10-minutes long).
- An on-going YouTube Series with a built-in audience.
- Press releases.

It's a full-on package that covers everything from the initial presentation through press releases to assure word gets out about the show even when it's in its infancy stage and even before it's officially sold to Hollywood.

Start with the Presentation Package

Like the other presentation packages with smaller budgets, it's mandatory to start with the presentation package. The Creator needs to get the logistics out of the way first while learning how to put together a show. If this is the Creator's first time putting a presentation package together, it won't be easy, but it'll be worth the hassle. Knowing what goes into a show can help the Creator later if and when problems arise.

Some Creators with higher budgets available might be tempted to pay someone to put this together for them. I'd advise the Creator to do it himself because that will assure that you're the one who knows and understands every logistical point in the series.

Go back over the following Chapters to review how to put the presentation package together:

- ➤ Determine the Show's Series Type (See Chapter Two)
- ➤ Put the presentation package together (See Chapter Three: Crafting the Reality-TV Show).
- ➤ Prepare the Presentation (See Chapter Four: Prepare a Reality-TV Presentation)
- ➤ Have a standard query letter ready to go (See Chapter Four: Prepare a Reality-TV Presentation)

Put Together a 1-3 Minute Trailer

After the Creator has put the presentation package together, it's time to do a trailer. Unlike the medium budget presentation package, the Creator can splurge on stock footage, music pieces, etc., but don't get too carried away. The trailer still needs to be quick and simplified. It doesn't have to look like a feature film trailer with elaborate, high-budget effects. In fact, I'd advise against this because it could make the show look too expensive to produce and reality-TV episodes are often done on shoestring budgets. However, the Creator can add more stock footage than the medium budget presentation. I'd also recommend sticking with one piece of music for the entire trailer. This gives the trailer a professional consistency.

To review the details on how to put a trailer together go to Chapter 5: The Reality-TV Show Creator, see section Understand Trailers and Sizzle Reels.

Also, the Creator can splurge on a longer trailer that runs up to 3-minutes, but be careful. Once again I must warn against making something that's so elaborate that the Creator's show looks too expensive to produce. In Hollywood, less is often better than more. The Creator can go beyond the 1-minute average run time, but exceeding 3-minutes means the Creator is telling too much of the story and breaking the Show, Don't Tell rule!

Create A Movie-Style Poster

Everyone has seen movie posters at the theaters, on billboards, etc. They're used to advertise a movie to an audience and consist of one poster with the movie's title, usually a shot of the actors in some type of action or dramatic moment that foreshadows the genre and a quick tagline that makes the audience yearn to see the movie.

The movie poster can be a powerful visual selling tool that can help the Creator gain the interest of a producer AND draw in an audience that will watch the trailer, sizzle reel and even become regulars for the show's YouTube Series! One simple poster can help the Creator land the audience required to make the reality-TV show sale.

But there's a catch! The poster the Creator is putting together isn't for a movie. It's for a TV show. The main difference is the actors. If the Creator has an on going, YouTube Series and can get a cool shot of the reality-TV stars for the cover, then great! If not, then the Creator will have to get creative!

For example, I once saw a TV show poster for a game show with only four lines that really sold the concept. The lines were in bright yellow against a black background with the title on the top. That was it, but it was provocative, memorable and helped land the Creator a lot of attention in Hollywood. Here's an example of what the TV poster for Survivor might appear like with only text:

SURVIVOR

15 Players

30 Days

1 Survivor

The Creator can do something like this for game shows, monster series, investigative series, etc. Or the Creator can go beyond this and add visuals, etc. Play with different posters to see which one grabs the viewer the most. How do you find out? Ask the Beta test audience's opinion when they come to see the trailer or view the sizzle reel. Have 2 or 3 sample posters ready and let them pick their favorite.

Adding reality-TV stars to the poster can get tricky if the series isn't sold yet or if the Creator doesn't have all the legal paperwork completed and owns the rights to exhibit their faces, voices, etc. (release forms). Stick with the basics for now and redo the poster later.

A Low-Budget Note

The Creator putting together a low-budget package might be able to swing a movie-style poster while putting together the reality-TV presentation package. After all, the Creator needs a COVER in the presentation package. Take extra time with the cover. All of it or a modified portion of it could become a movie-style poster that the Creator can use on websites, Facebook, etc.

Create the Sizzle Reel

Lately, sizzle reels are all the talk of the town and most Creators presenting their second or third shows for consideration have sizzle reels. They are not required for the aspiring Creator, but many are doing them nowadays so they look like a Hollywood player when they walk in the door.

The sizzle reel differs from the trailer in several ways; it's longer usually running up to 10-minutes, goes more-in depth about the project and tends to be a little less flashy and hyped than the trailer. In other words, it's more down-to-earth, but be careful that it doesn't become boring with overdone interviews or long scenes taken from the on-going series. Use the trailer's fast-paced selling points to put the sizzle reel together, pausing at just the right intervals to highlight certain things then move back into the selling mode.

To review the details of the sizzle reel, which is very similar to putting together the trailer, see Chapter 5: The Reality-TV Show Creator, see section Understand Trailers and Sizzle Reels.

The sizzle reels cost should be fully explored before taking on this part of the presentation. The extra stock footage, music rights, and reality-TV star interviews might seem like they'll only cost a little bit extra, but the Creator needs to take into consider the additional length of the sizzle reel means more minutes to edit and that can substantially increase the overall costs.

Create the On-Going YouTube Series

For those who have the financial resources this will seem like the dream part of the presentation because the Creator can actually begin filming and airing the show before it's sold!

This can get tricky because if the Creator has no experience filming a TV show, things can go south really fast. First, I'd advise the Creator, regardless of available budget, to keep things simple and cost effective. If the Creator has to hire a full, union filming crew with all the perks, then it's way overboard. Remember, shows like *Ghost Adventures* is filmed with three guys who have their own cameras with built-in microphones. They film each other then have it edited by industry professionals. That's it! Shows that started out as web series have used similar, low-budget tactics when filming the web series.

This isn't just so the Creator can save money. It's to prove the show can be shot for a budget that's consistent with reality-TV's lower budgeted market. Start by renting or using a one-camera (professional Hollywood style) and a sound boom (and hire someone who knows how to do sound). This should be enough. This is often referred to as a *skeleton crew* with one camera, one cameraman, a sound boom guy and the reality-TV stars.

It can also get tricky when it comes to the reality-TV stars that will appear on the show. Lets face it, they may not want to participate until the show's been sold and they have a guaranteed salary. This can quickly sink the prospect of doing an on-going series, but if the Creator is lucky enough to have reality-TV stars willing to do a few episodes for free, then go for it.

Word of Caution: I wouldn't advise getting into a situation where the Creator owes deferred payments for the web series. This can hurt contract talks with studios, unions and show runners later. Make sure the reality-TV cast knows (in writing) that this is being done for promotional purposes ONLY and any and all compensation they might receive would be contingent upon the show selling to a network. In other words, no money until the show sells and the money is generated from future TV episodes with no funds being paid for the web series. Also, remind the cast that the web series isn't likely to ever air on TV and that the pilot episode and subsequent episodes would have to be filmed after the sale, which would include pay that's contingent upon studio negotiations and vary per show.

Web Series Episodes

The Creator should really sit down and think through the series before plunging into the deep waters. How many episodes can the Creator financially handle? If it's only one, then this isn't a web series – it's a pilot! Shooting only the pilot episode is a waste of time in reality-TV because this episode is never going to air, show runners will probably tighten up the format and it may not be enough to bring in an audience.

Only go for the web series if the Creator can do a minimum of 3 episodes, often referred to as a *block*! If the Creator can do more that's fantastic, but remember the goal isn't to create a forever-running web series, it's to sell the concept to a network!

When the Creator decides on how many episodes, make sure to advertise it on the poster and on YouTube. Stay Tuned for a 3-part web series....

Keep the series limited in duration. Just because the presentation package indicates the show will run for 30-minutes or 1-hour doesn't obligate the Creator to film a web series of the same length. In fact, I'd advocate against it. It's just a waste of time and money. Do short films for each episode that run around 10-15 minutes. This is what the *Dead Files* did before the Travel Channel picked them up and the show became a hit series. Cut into the heart of the episode, present the concept/story and get out! I believe the old *Dead Files* web series are still available for viewing on YouTube. Watch them and then compare with the finished 1-hour show. It's a great how-to example and the Creator can see the changes that were made to really give the finished, 1-hour show a polished TV look.

Besides the skeleton camera crew, the Creator will need to hire a professional film editor, no exceptions. It's okay to make a fun trailer at home or to hire a high school or college student to do it for you, but this is a web series that requires the sharp eye of an experienced editor who knows how to put everything filmed together in a way that makes it look professionally polished. Obviously, this is going to cost the Creator time and money. While the Creator might have went out and shot the episodes in a few weeks, it could take months of editing before the web series is ready for uploading as a web series on YouTube.

This could create a problem if the Creator began advertising the web series debut date and the project is still being edited (post production). To help prevent this issue, wait until the episodes are filmed, then get an estimated completion date from the editor after he/she has viewed the footage and discussed the look/feel of the project with the Creator. Give an extra 2-weeks past the date the editor gave as a due date to provide a cushion should things go wrong (like having to go back and film some things again) or the editing gets behind schedule.

When the episodes are ready to go, advertise the web series anywhere you can; blogs, Facebook, Instagram, word-of-mouth, paid ads, etc. Use the trailer to help hype the web series and get the word out. Upload the trailer to Facebook and announce the date and time when the first episode will air. DO NOT upload the entire web series episode to Facebook or anywhere except YouTube. That's overkill and defeats the purpose of doing a web series in the first place, which includes getting the audience to view the series on YouTube where the audience # can be counted!

Ask viewers to SUBSCRIBE to the web series, then send them announcements about upcoming episodes and ask them to share the information with their social media network.

Don't get so wrapped up and excited with making the web series that you forget the primary objective: to sell the series to a network! For that, the Creator needs to show they have built an audience of 200,000 or more who watch the show when it airs. Try to keep the airtime consistent. Maybe the show airs once a week on the same day at the same time. I wouldn't recommend spreading it out too far, like months in between episodes. Audiences tend to have a short attention span and may not remember the series two or three months down the road. That's why I advocated having all the episodes filmed and ready to go before airing them as a series. Also, don't bundle them up where they can all be seen at once. Treat the web series like a real network show that only airs once a week at the same set time and date, but with a new show. However, it's okay to leave the old shows on the channel for viewers.

The Built-In Audience

Once the Creator's episodes reach the magic 200,000 viewing audience, it's time to market to producers and lead with this: MY SHOW HAS 200K AUDIENCE MEMBERS!

Add a blurb to the movie poster. Add it to the trailer and the presentation package. If the Creator's pitched the project to producers in the past and they've passed, revisit these producers with an update on the show's status. They might decide they want to take a second look, which could result in a sale!

Spread the word on social media, blogs, Twitter, etc., and now it's time to do a press release.

Press Release

Yes, that's right! The Creator can purchase a press release for the show even when it hasn't sold yet! Forget paying for expensive advertising. A press release can be far less money and generate some real heat for the project. Do an on-line search to compare pricing for press releases and see which companies offer the best options for the release, like which newspapers, magazines, website will the release appear? Who writes it? Will you get to review and edit the release before it goes out?

The Creator can't do this until the show reaches an on-line audience level or the Creator will look like a fool. Yes, I know books often have press releases BEFORE they hit the market, but that's an entirely different market than a TV show, and usually only done for book authors with established names and large followings.

The Creator must wait until the web series has gathered some real heat and has a viable viewing audience. The press release will be to announce it as the next big thing....

....of course, this could backfire and the web series may never sell to a network, but it can also be worth the risks.

An extra note: YouTube Web Series can come with built-in advertising dollars that encourage the Creator to stay in this medium, provide content and reap all the financial rewards without bothering to take the show to a wider TV audience. That's up to the Creator, but be sure to explore all options or just sell the licensing rights to the networks and continue to run the web series, if the studio contract allows it.

Or the Creator could use the advertising dollars from YouTube to finance their own network show. Studios love a show that comes in fully packaged that they don't have to pay for. It means less risk for them, but it doesn't mean the Creator gets to keep all the creative rights. The studio will still want the show to adhere to its airing requirements, which could mean changes in format, casting, etc. Be flexible and agree to their terms. Don't take it personal or the Creator will ruin the chance to get the show on the air. Think of it in these terms – the studios are a billion dollar a year business, so they must be doing something right. This is your first show! Who's more likely to know what's best for the series?

Final Word

While I don't advocate marketing the series to a producer before the Hollywood Pitch Presentation is ready, which is determined by the Creator's budget, if the Creator has put together a web series, there's no reason why the Creator can't invite producers to view the on-going series even before it reaches a certain audience level.

This isn't without risks because the producer will keep checking back to see if the series made the required count. If it does meet the audience count, the Creator will have an interested producer ready to talk a deal. If not, the producer may consider the Creator's ideas a bust and blacklist him or her for future consideration. Yes, this is a tough and competitive business.

I'd only suggest doing this if the Beta test audience numbers were extremely high, like a 90% favorable rating. The Creator should Beta test audience the episodes before airing them! Always Beta test! Getting feedback is imperative in any creative endeavor to assure the Creator isn't just meeting the terms of his or her own creative needs, but has become flexible enough to bend to the audience's expectations.

Bonus: The Investor Factor

The book doesn't really discuss raising investor funds to cover the expenses of a reality-TV show presentation, especially at the higher budgeted level. Most Creators can raise the necessary funds themselves or stick with a presentation that suits their individual budget needs. The Creator can use his/her own funds, put everything on a credit card for a deferred payment or even start an on-line fund raising effort (although this could entail giving away perks the Creator may want to keep).

There are shows that have outside funders meaning outside the studio/producer system, like *Finding Bigfoot*. Studios like these shows because it lessens their financial risks. But it increases the risks to the Creator who will have to share his or her portion of the profits with the investor, usually at a pretty high rate, often leaving the Creator with as little as a 20% ownership in his own show! Yes, it happens more often than not. Plus, the investor becomes the

Executive Producer (money man) of the show and that's a powerful position that can make hiring and firing decisions that can often overrule the Creator. In other words, does the Creator want this person overseeing everything? If the answer is NO, then stick with the presentation package that fits the Creator's budget and do NOT accept investor funds, even if offered! The temptation isn't worth the long-term hassle.

Without the investor's involvement, the Creator only has to work with the producer and studio. And, mostly importantly will still have creative control and the clout to do the hiring and firing. Plus, the Creator will keep a much larger portion of the profits and isn't that why the Creator started doing this in the first place?

Investors will probably be sending me hate mail, but this book is written with the Creator in mind and promised the Creator that he/she could put together a reality-TV presentation to submit to Hollywood with $0 up to a high budget based on the Creator's current bank account and that doesn't require an investor!

CHAPTER SEVEN

MARKET THE REALITY-TV SHOW

This book teaches the Creator how to come up with an idea and create a presentation based on a specific budget in order to have a strong market product to pitch to Hollywood. The book has shown that the Creator can be an established film/TV writer or a bartender from Philadelphia. Reality-TV doesn't scrutinize who you are, but whether the show can deliver an audience or not.

The book also provides specifics on must-haves based on budget requirements starting from $0 budgets up to high budgets.

The chapters covered a variety of marketing techniques so this Chapter might seem like an overview, but I recommend going through it again so the Creator doesn't overlook any prospects for a sale.

First, make sure that everything is DONE before proceeding to market, as outlined in this book. Cutting corners will only cost the Creator in the long run. All of the marketing techniques covered in this chapter can be used in a variety of ways and some may need to be left out due to budget constraints.

❖ THE SOCIAL MEDIA PLATFORM

Before presenting the package to a producer, get the project setup on social media and start building hype. Post it on Facebook and upload the trailer, if applicable. Use the movie-style poster for websites, Facebook, etc. Have the first web series (if applicable) ready to air. Have all of this prepared and ready to go BEFORE soliciting producers.

In previous chapters, we talked about the vital importance of building a YouTube audience of 200,000 viewers or more. While I don't advocate soliciting to producers until the Creator's reached the golden #, there's no reason the Creator can't use the increasing audience # to promote the series on Facebook, etc. Every time the show reaches a new landmark, like every 50,000 viewers, post it to Facebook and ask your friends to share it. This could easily help the Creator double or triple the audience size.

❖ MARKET TO PRODUCERS

Start by using the IMDB Pro list (Reality-TV Producers) the Creator put together earlier. Send the producer a sales letter, which was previously discussed in this book.

Once the show hits the 200,000 viewers mark in regards to the combined audience between the trailer, sizzle reel and/or the web series, it's time to announce this benchmark to every producer in town! Send out a blanketed email via a service or painstakingly do it manually, but be aware an email coming from such a script blaster service might end up in a producer's SPAM folder.

Note: If the Creator has a trailer, sizzle reel and/or web series, all three DO NOT have to reach the 200,000 before marketing. Only ONE of them has to reach that number!

The bolder Creator can invite the producer to view the series episodes, but this is risky because the producer will follow-up to see if the show has generated an audience or not. Best advice is to wake for the golden number, then shout it from the rooftops.

❖ THE DIY APPROACH

The do-it-yourself approach technically applies to most of this book, but for the purpose of this chapter, it'll include marketing via websites, festivals and word of mouth.

First, as previously discussed there are website where the Creator can pitch the reality-TV show, for a fee, to producers. The sites include www.VirtualPitchFest.com, www.TVWritersVault.com and www.inktip.com. The main reason to avoid these would be costs, but if the writer can swing the extra expense, it's a great way to market, but DO NOT make it the only alternative since I believe the best route is doing the required legwork on IMDB and blanket market to producers who may not be listed on the websites noted above.

Local festivals, arts & crafts festivals and even music festivals, where they allow vendor booths, are a good DIY place to market the show. This might seem like a long shot, especially since a producer may never show up here, but building the show's audience, hype and interest is well worth the money. And the Creator might be surprised when they run into someone who knows a Hollywood producer!

Word-of-mouth is probably the most powerful of all advertisers regardless of what a person is selling. It always has been and always will be. You mentioned you're looking to buy a new car and ten of your friends offer an opinion. That's the way life works. Same with movies, TV shows and reality-TV shows. If someone comes to a festival and watches the trailer and loved it, they'll tell their friends, family and co-workers about it. Soon the Creator will have hundreds of extra people flocking to see it on-line and this will help bring the Creator closer to the 200,000 viewing audience's golden number!

NOTE: There's no timeframe for reaching the 200,000-viewer mark. The Creator could have reached the mark in a single weekend or a year. What's important is that you've reached it and the Creator now has bragging rights to his/her own audience that likes and/or follows their reality-TV show.

❖ TROUBLESHOOT MARKETING

What if the Creator has done everything in this book and still hasn't sold the reality-TV show?

If it's a zero budget package, the Creator may have to bring in a friend to help pay for a few additives to give the package a visual jumpstart. Don't make the friend a partner, just take a short-term loan or put the trailer $ on a credit card. Hold a yard sale or an on-line fundraiser to get the cash. Up the game and increase the chances of a sale.

If it's a medium budget package, did the Creator run it through the Beta test audience? I'd bet the answer is NO. The Creator slid right past this part thinking they had this down pat, when in reality the Creator's presentation is lacking in some way. STOP! Go back and bring in the Beta test audience. Find out what's wrong and fix it!

If it's a high budget package, the most likely culprit is that something is overdone and it's scared off producers who think the show will cost too much to produce on a weekly basis. Really scrutinize areas where the project's been overdone. Does the 2-minute trailer have huge special effects that need edited out to give the show a low-budget look and feel? Is the cast costs too high, like a celebrity who wants big bucks? Is the sizzle reel overdone, running over 10 minutes or does the reel bore the viewer? Take a good hard look and if the Creator still doesn't see anything wrong, ask for outside advice from a pro, like an agent, manager, producer or screenwriter. Get their advice and take it. Or go back to square one and bring in a new beta audience to review the entire package and give opinions.

Confusion is a factor I've often found that holds up a concept from becoming a reality-TV show. The producer simply doesn't get it. The game show rules are too complex or contrived. Again, this is where the Beta test audience can really help stop the Creator from making the mistake of marketing the project before it's ready.

No spin factor! Earlier chapters discuss that the Creator can pitch the industry with a concept that is currently on TV, like shows about Bigfoot, but the sale won't happen unless the show has enough unique qualities to stand out against existing shows. Again, a Beta Test audience can help a Creator determine if it's too much like another show and help the Creator change up enough factors to make it unique. Before the beta audience views your presentation package, ask them to watch the competing show and make a comparison. This can help the Creator weed out areas where the show is too much like its competitor and help the Creator and a unique spin.

The budget breaks the bank. The Creator's picked a concept, location or cast/celebrity with such high filming costs involved that it would far exceed the limited weekly budget of a reality-TV show. Go back over this book for ways to reduce the budget and keep the show's quality high while maintaining a reasonable budget.

The show's outdated. Most Creators know better, but I have seen this. Nobody wants to watch a nostalgic show on how to create timepieces. If the Creator is truly obsessed with timepieces, then find a modern way to uniquely present it to an audience. Maybe travel the world discovering timepieces and what they've meant to humans throughout history. Entertain us or the show will never sell!

The show is too far ahead of its time. Dark Matter is an example. It's a fascinating subject science is just beginning to explore, but there isn't enough material to explore the concept in a long-running reality-TV series. Producers want shows that will be around for the long haul.

The show is boring! This book discusses factors that can make a show seem boring, like lackluster reality-TV stars, a poorly thought-out concept, failure to discover if an audience would even want to see the show on TV. If the Creator isn't sure about the concept up front, then do an early Beta test audience where the Creator sends out questionnaires for people to fill out to determine if they'd like the type of show the Creator wants to pitch to Hollywood. The Creator will need an 80% or higher positive response before proceeding to put a presentation package together. If the Creator gets a rating, then it's time to move on to the next idea.

Finally, the show might need a fresh spin to make it work. Watching a show regarding a House of Cats isn't quite as interesting as watching *My Cat From Hell*. The Creator might have the right idea, but the way the idea's presented might need some work. Keep at it and keep marketing!

❖ FINAL WORD

A Hollywood screenwriter was driving along the 10-freeway in Los Angeles headed toward Las Vegas when off in the middle of the remote desert he saw a cargo plane unloading men in orange jumpsuits. He stopped at the nearest diner and discovered the details of the mysterious plane and its occupants and then went on to write the hit movie CON AIR starring Nicolas Cage.

Ideas for movies, TV and reality-TV are all around us. We often tend to drive through life missing the golden opportunities. Slow down and really take a look around. If you've lived in a rural area for 20 years and often wondered where that unfinished road leads, then find out! If you've driven past a strange warehouse in the city for years that has no windows, no signs, but always has cars out front, then discover what it is (with caution!).

For the more adventurous, purchase a hard copy map of your area within a 2-4 hour driving distance. Take a good look at it and mark towns you've never heard of, then research those towns and plan a day trip to drive through, being sure to stop at a local eatery to ask questions. You'll discover a whole new world right in your own backyard. A world where you might find the next hit reality-TV show!

Sincerely,
Barb Doyon
Owner/Founder
Extreme Screenwriting
www.extremescreenwriting.com

74060048R00082

Made in the USA
San Bernardino, CA
13 April 2018